d by John Deere Tractor

ober 18-1927   443

"How could anyone at all interested in the history, culture, mechanics of agriculture ignore the remarkable role of John Deere green? The John Deere has become almost a transcendent, universal icon for the phrase 'old tractor.'"
—Roger Welsch

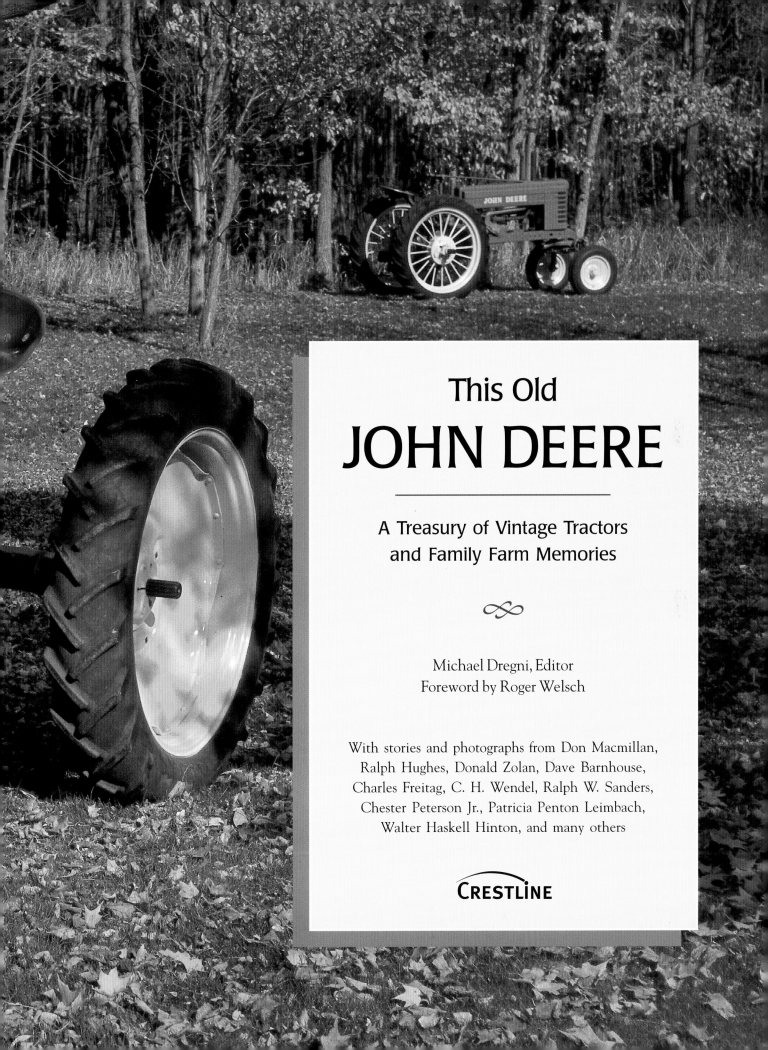

This Old
JOHN DEERE

A Treasury of Vintage Tractors and Family Farm Memories

Michael Dregni, Editor
Foreword by Roger Welsch

With stories and photographs from Don Macmillan,
Ralph Hughes, Donald Zolan, Dave Barnhouse,
Charles Freitag, C. H. Wendel, Ralph W. Sanders,
Chester Peterson Jr., Patricia Penton Leimbach,
Walter Haskell Hinton, and many others

CRESTLINE

This edition published in 2013 by CRESTLINE
a division of BOOK SALES, INC.
276 Fifth Avenue Suite 206
New York, New York 10001 USA

This edition published by arrangement with Voyageur Press, Inc.
400 First Avenue North, Suite 400, Minneapolis, Minnesota, 55401

Edited by Michael Dregni
Designed by Andrea Rud
Printed in China

10 9 8 7 6 5 4 3 2 1

Library of Congress Cataloging-in-Publication Data
This old John Deere: a treasury of vintage tractors and family farm memories / Michael Dregni, editor; foreword by Roger Welsch.
   p.cm.
  ISBN 978-0-7858-3005-4
  1. John Deere tractors—United States—History. 2. John Deere tractors—Unites States—Ancecdotes. 3. Farm tractors—United States—History. 4. Farm tractors—United States—Anecdotes. I. Dregni, Michael, 1961–
  S711.T477 2002
  631.3' 72—dc21

                    2002002646

On the endpapers: *A Johnny Popper pulls a Holt combine across the Canadian prairies. (Glenbow Archives)*

On the frontispiece: *Kitty rests on the front end of a 1959 John Deere Model 730 Diesel. Owner: Dick Bockwoldt. (Photograph © Ralph W. Sanders)*

On the title pages: *John Deere Model HWH. Owners: Walter and Bruce Keller. (Photograph © Andy Kraushaar)*

On these pages: *A Johnny Popper and its Deere combine stop to empty grain into a waiting truck. (Photograph © J. C. Allen & Son)*

Opposite the contents page: *A 1944 John Deere Model A. Owner: Joe Joas. (Photograph © Andy Kraushaar)*

Acknowledgments

I would like to thank all of the people who helped bring this book to life: John O. Allen and his family's incredible photographic legacy; Keith Baum; Tom Benda, Apple Creek Publishing; Richard Hain, *Green Magazine*; Ralph Hughes; Justin Isherwood; Andy Kraushaar; Patricia Penton Leimbach; Don Macmillan; Colleen McCarty-Gould; Chester Peterson Jr.; Kim Pratt; Ralph W. Sanders; Gary W. Schmidt and Chris Hansen, Hadley Liscencing; Orlan Skare; Chuck Wendel; Bird Vincent; Jennifer Zolan, Zolan Fine Arts; and last but far from least, Roger Welsch.

Finally, my thanks to everyone at Voyageur Press.

Contents

John Deere Green

By Roger Welsch

Roger Welsch appears on CBS TV's *Sunday Morning* program, spreading the word about old barns, farm living, and vintage tractors wherever the airwaves travel. His writings on vintage tractors appear regularly in *Successful Farming* magazine's "Ageless Iron" section, as well as in *Esquire*, *Smithsonian*, and *Nebraska Farmer*. In addition, he is the author of more than twenty books, including *Old Tractors Never Die*, also published by Voyageur Press.

I read somewhere that when the British General John "Gentleman Johnny" Burgoyne surrendered his entire army to American General Horatio Gates in the turning point of our Revolutionary War, the British military band present at the surrender played the tune "The World Turned Upside Down." It simply made no sense, this group of upstart ragamuffins accepting the surrender of the finest army in the world. Sometimes things make no sense and everything flies in the face of logic.

I can imagine a lot of people reading the cover credits on this book and thinking pretty much the same thing. *This Old John Deere* with a foreword by Roger Welsch? What sense does that make? The world has been turned upside down. Roger Welsch—unashamed of public photographs showing him lovingly embracing *Sweet Allis*, the first of his fleet of more than thirty Persian Orange Allis-Chalmers tractors—now penning a tribute to—*gasp, choke!*—one of those Greenies! Is it possible?!

Old-Time Green
Combining wheat in the summer of 1940 with a Johnny Popper and Deere harvester. (Photograph © J. C. Allen & Son)

Some of you will be even more aghast because you know my preference for Persian Orange was reinforced during the spring of 2000 when I was run down from behind by—what else?!—a John Deere tractor. I was walking along a quiet gravel street in the town of Dannebrog, Nebraska, on the left side of the road as law and good sense dictate, bringing home the mail on my daily stroll, when suddenly a John Deere sprang out from behind a tree, knocked me down, threw me into the ditch, broke my left hand and some ribs, and stood triumphantly over me as the Dannebrog EMTs checked me over for injuries and picked gravel and burs out of my hair. (I explained to them that they could just let *that* go since it was actually residue from my walk home from the tavern the night before.)

As if the humiliation of being downed by a Deere—from behind!—was not enough, for weeks afterward I had to endure the jibes and taunts of my cronies. One wise-acre cracked that it was my fault since I was not wearing a slow-moving-vehicle triangle. A rumor circulated that I had been chasing cars and snapping at tires. Again. Even Wife Linda announced that she was asking the farmer who owned the machine to "put it down" since she had heard that once a Deere tastes blood, it is never quite the same.

And there you are. They were all joking, of course, even though my injuries turned out to be fairly serious: Six months later, I am still recovering from the broken hand. But for the purposes of these pages the issue is that everyone joked with me about the instrument of my injuries—a John Deere—because they knew that my love of old tractors is, not even far below the surface, color blind.

I believe that's true of most of us lovers of old iron. Our enchantment is with old machines, historic tractors, rusty iron. Even if our hearts run to one color or another, or one era above another, or one mechanical configuration—think of the ferocious devotion of those who embrace two cylinders!—the reality is that any rivalries, any disputation about one tractor being faster, bigger, stronger, or prettier than another is just so much coffee-table joking.

John Deere Green
Never underestimate the appeal of a 1939 John Deere Model B. Owners: Del and Don Endres. (Photograph © Andy Kraushaar)

The fact of the matter is, most of us have come to our preferences by accident. Maybe your father's first tractor was a Minneapolis-Moline. Perhaps there was an Oliver dealer nearby. Or maybe your own first tractor was an almost accidental purchase of a real bargain at a farm sale.

In my case, a friend told me he had an old tractor he would *give* me. It had been parked for two years in a woodlot in a town not far from Lincoln, Nebraska. I don't recall that he even said what kind it was. I don't recall that I knew what it was even when I saw it, having never sat on a tractor seat before in my life. But it was a 1937 Allis-Chalmers Model WC, and suddenly I was an Orangeman.

It could have been otherwise. Boy, could it have been otherwise! Not long before *Sweet Allis* came into my life, a neighbor told me he had a John Deere Model B he would sell me if I needed a tractor. $100. Runs fine. Can you imagine how many times I have kicked myself for not taking him up on that offer?! And I would have been a Greenie, just like that.

Almost every one of my tractor buddies is a John Deere man. It would have been easy to be a Greenie. My father-in-law Jake has a John Deere Model B. I suspect that if he had sensed I could use it here, he would have gladly let me have it—at least for a little while—and that too would have led me down the road to becoming a Greenie.

In fact, because of Jake's long association with his B, Wife Linda has a soft spot in her heart for Green Bs too. This means that there are currently four pretty shaggy John Deere B's sitting in our machine yard, which in turn means that I take plenty of flak from my friends in town—again, with the constant understanding that whatever our trivial preferences, our basic affection is simply for old tractors.

Need more proof of my sincerity here? I got it. At the very moment I write these, totally unbeknownst to Linda, I have bought a gorgeously restored John Deere B for her. I have a big red bow here in my office that I'll put on the grill when I drive it into the yard and give it to her. How is that going to go over? Well, hopefully better than the Christmas I gave her a real nice shotgun!

Moreover, I am a historian of sorts. Anyone who works with old machinery is—and has to be! How could anyone at all interested in the history, culture, mechanics of agriculture ignore the remarkable role of John Deere green? And how could anyone who understands America's love of tractors overlook the incredible affection we all have for John Deere? Let's face it: Green is the very backbone of American farm machinery, from the earliest innovations like the steel plow to the overwhelming plurality of John Deere collectors, restorers, and scholars swirling around those of us who love old iron. The John Deere has become almost a transcendent, universal icon for the phrase "old tractor." John Deere green has become as American as red, white, and blue.

For those of us who love old iron, the surrender is almost complete. Even those dedicated to Oliver green, International red, or Allis orange, now have to admit that the American tractor is John Deere. (You can't imagine how hard it is for me to put that down in print—and I can only imagine and anticipate the shouts of derision and denial that comment will generate, but the truth is now beyond proving!) I and many others are still heretics, rebels, anarchists, crazies, outlaws. We find our pleasures in other colors. But the passion, numbers, and persistence of John Deere tractors are undeniable.

I wrote above that that assertion of John Deere dominance is "beyond proving." What is the evidence of that? Well, I look out among my own machinery—my beloved Allises—and see the four green John Deere Model Bs. And I wonder at and consider the magic of two cylinders. I have no idea why two cylinders are somehow more—what? magical?—than four, but it's true.

You know, the time might still come when I find the courage to dig into one of those bucket-size cylinders and try to discover what makes them work, just as I did, in utter ignorance and innocence, ten years ago when I first opened the brake cover on *Sweet Allis* and was infected by the incurable disease of Rustophilia, the love of old iron. Could I catch the green disease? It's not beyond the realm of possibility.

1949 John Deere Model AO
Owner: Augie Scoto. (Photograph by Hans Halberstadt)

And what's that I hear? Yep, it's my pal Dick Day. And he's coming into the yard with—Oh boy! Isn't that pretty?—Linda's John Deere B. I'll pull one of my Allises out into the sun and snow so there is a place for her B in the shed. I'm still an Allis man, but it would be silly to deny the beauty, magic, and history of that pretty green machine.

Why would I give Linda a John Deere B and not an Allis-Chalmers WC? Because I love her, through it all.

And because all of us—even the Persian Oranges—have to love a John Deere. Through it all.

"Golden Harvest"
John Deere tractors harvest gold in this painting by artist Dave Barnhouse. (Artwork © Dave Barnhouse/Hadley Licensing)

This Old John Deere

I first sat behind the steering wheel of a John Deere tractor when I was eight years old. As much as I wanted to believe that I was actually driving that big green machine, I was in truth sitting in my father's lap and was secretly happy to have his big, strong hands there to grab ahold of the steering wheel should anything go amiss. My short legs also did not reach to the floor, and so he was in control there, too. All I was really doing was playing farmer, but it was a fine fantasy.

It's a game many a farmkid has played—and with good reason. That feeling of "driving" a John Deere, sitting perched high above the fields on a sunny summer day and looking out as far as one can see over the tops of the cornstalks, makes a young farm boy or girl feel not only like a true farmer, but like a king or queen.

A John Deere tractor was not just a machine. The Johnny Popper replaced the horse on many a farm, and like Old Dobbin, farmers came to rely on that green tractor. Many farmers still remember their first sight of one of the newfangled mechanical mules. Some still remember the day their favorite horse team was traded in for the seemingly cold-blooded steel machinery as a new way of life came to pass down on the farm. But over time, those farmers worked side by side with their Deere, day after day, year after year. They developed a relationship of trust and reliance and respect and ultimately affection for that machine.

Over the years, the John Deere became almost like part of the family. It appeared in the family photo album, family stories, family memories. Farm folk remembered history by the year a child was born, by a season of a bumper crop or a drought, and by the day a new John Deere arrived on the farm.

1937 John Deere Model AOS
Owners: Walter, Bruce, and Jason Keller. (Photograph © Andy Kraushaar)

Memories are what this book is all about. *This Old John Deere* is a treasury of memories—short stories, essays, tall tales, and reminiscences—devoted to John Deere machines and their role on the family farm. The stories are at times worshipful of a family's beloved Poppin' Johnny. At other times, they are rambling rants about a tractor that didn't pull its weight on the farm or long-recalled curses about learning to drive tractor, remembered vividly, even now, decades after the guilty party has been retired to rust in peace in a windbreak or scrapyard. Whatever the case, all of the stories are nostalgic, sentimental, and sometimes humorous, and all pay homage to the machine that created a revolution in world agriculture.

The authors of the pieces collected in this anthology come from a wide range of backgrounds and a variety of farming regions. Some are respected tractor historians, others are regular farm folk with a story to share. Among the well-known historians are Don Macmillan, Ralph Hughes, Ralph W. Sanders, C. H. Wendel, and Chester Peterson Jr. Other authors include Patricia Penton Leimbach, Justin Isherwood, Orlan Skare, Bruce Bair, Bird Vincent, Colleen McCarthy-Gould, and Kim Pratt. In addition, there is a foreword from everyone's favorite tractor philosopher and funnyman, Roger Welsch.

The photography come from a variety of well-known photographers and archives, including Ralph W. Sanders, Andy Kraushaar, Keith Baum, and others, including the magnificent record of American farm life found in the archives of J. C. Allen & Son.

In addition, there are paintings and other farm art from Donald Zolan, Charles Freitag, Dave Barnhouse, Walter Haskell Hinton, and others.

In the end, this book was designed to be part history of the John Deere, part tribute, and part just good fun. Enjoy.

Michael Dregni

Yuletide Green
Decked in lights and a fresh layer of snow, a styled John Deere Model A in Michigan spreads holiday cheer. (Photograph © Keith Baum)

CHAPTER I

Lore and Legend of the Poppin' Johnnies

"Tractors changed everything. Never mind the rest of the world counted time as B.C. or A.D., for agriculture the ages were either B.T. or A.T., Before Tractor or After. Never mind no one else understood, the farmer did."
—Justin Isherwood, "Tractors," *Book of Plough*

In the beginning, there was Iowa thresherman John Froelich's tractor, the pioneering gas-powered tractor that was capable of propelling itself forward and backward. Froelich's machine was the forerunner of the Waterloo Boy, which in turn became the John Deere Model D.

From the Waterloo Boy, Deere inherited the simplicity of the two-cylinder engine. And so beloved was the sound of those Deere twins that their sound gave birth to a nickname that farm folk still affectionately know them by: Poppin' Johnnies.

"The Barn Raising"
Three youngsters use a John Deere as a hideout to eat blueberry pie behind while the barn-raising work goes on in this painting by Iowa artist Charles Freitag. (Apple Creek Publishing)

Recollections of the Early Days of John Deere Tractors

By C. H. Wendel

Chuck Wendel is without doubt one of the most famous and prolific tractor historians in the world. He was a pioneer in writing about the farm tractor's history, a job which has taken him throughout the United States, Canada, and Europe. He has authored thirty-some books, several of which will be recognized by any tractor fan: the famous *Encyclopedia of American Farm Tractors*, *Massey Tractors* covering Canada's finest, *150 Years of J. I. Case*, *150 Years of International Harvester*, *The Allis-Chalmers Story*, *Unusual Vintage Tractors*, and more.

In these recollections, Chuck shares some favorite farm tractor yarns about Deere's history and his own family history with Deere machines.

The Good Old Days
A 1940s farmer pauses with a big smile on his face while driving his John Deere Model A.
(Photograph © J. C. Allen & Son)

Deere & Company started out in the 1830s with John Deere's steel plow, the ultimate primary tillage implement. The company continued building a wide range of tillage implements until finally diversifying into other machines about 1900. For example, the John Deere Grain Binder saw first light in 1910; John Deere combines came out about 1927. The John Deere threshing machines finally appeared in 1929 when the company bought out Wagner-Langemo Company of Minneapolis. Subsequently, Deere built several different thresher models.

Deere was intensely interested in putting a tractor on the market, even before World War I. At the time, there were literally hundreds of companies in the tractor market. All but a few came and went within twenty years or so. Competition forced a lot of them out of business, whereas others simply didn't have a tractor that farmers wanted. In those days, many manufacturers followed the theory of build-

ing what they thought the farmer *needed*, not necessarily what farmers *wanted*. Thus, it was nearly impossible to market some of these designs, even though they might have come from a large company with a large advertising budget.

Another problem was that tractor manufacturers of the pre–World War I period were selling way too much iron for way too little money. Couple this with crop failures or a glitch in the farmer's income, and companies like M. Rumely were forced into reorganization to re-emerge as the Advance-Rumely Thresher Company. Then there is the famous story of the Bull tractor: Here was a design that certainly heralded the beginning of small, lightweight tractors. The problem was that this first design left plenty of room for better designs, and despite early success, competition from other tractor companies forced the Bull off the market.

Then there were the charlatans. Appealing to

that human resource of greed, they offered stock in a "proposed tractor concern" that sometimes existed only in the imagination of the promoters. The result was that thousands of investors lost their money in these schemes. There were others who really intended to build a tractor, but hoped they could raise enough money from the sale of stock to launch the company. Oftentimes this never happened at all, or the company might have hand-built a few prototypes to give the appearance of honesty and propriety. The result was that farmers soon came to view many of these firms with a jaundiced eye, and even had their suspicions about some of the larger, established firms.

Everyone acquainted with the tractor business became keenly aware of the Fordson tractor when it was first announced in 1916. Henry Ford appealed directly to farmers, selling the Fordson through the same agencies that sold his famous Model T auto-

At Work

A John Deere Model D and Deere binder cut wheat in the 1930s. (Photograph © J. C. Allen & Son)

mobile. Although the Fordson had its problems, it was perhaps more than any other tractor responsible for eliminating many inferior designs. The competition provided by the Fordson also goaded competing companies, especially International Harvester, to come up with new and improved designs that could successfully compete with the Fordson.

The Fordson had its own set of problems, despite its popularity. About 1917 the United States Department of Agriculture sent Professor Arnold Yerkes from Washington, D. C. to the Fordson factories. The Yerkes Report on the Fordson was unfavorable in several aspects, yet apparently the USDA decided to suppress his report. That almost guaranteed that it would meet the public, and it did, in several different magazines of the day. The ensuing flap created a lot of news at the time, but apparently did nothing to blunt the overwhelming sales of the Fordson.

The turbulent times in the tractor business in, the 1912–1920 period saw numerous designs that would not perform as claimed, if indeed they would perform anywhere near the glowing claims of the manufacturer or the salesman. This eventually led to the Nebraska Tractor Test Law, which required all tractors sold in Nebraska to be tested at a new Tractor Test Laboratory. If they didn't pass the test, the tractors had to be modified so they would pass, and if that didn't work, they could not be sold in Nebraska. Almost immediately, farmers across the United States began to look at Nebraska Test results before buying a tractor. Upon passage of this law, virtually everyone who was building tractors submitted samples to the Tractor Test Laboratory.

In retrospect, this law had a huge impact on the tractor industry, especially since it brought stability and trustworthiness to small and large manufacturers alike. There are probably few state laws passed anywhere in the United States that have had such a profound effect on a national basis.

Against all this background, Deere & Company quietly sat back and continued various tractor

1924 Waterloo Boy Model N
Owner: Jim Russell. (Photograph © Ralph W. Sanders)

experiments, none of which ever went to market. The company simply wasn't satisfied with promoting a design that it felt was not what the farmer wanted or needed.

Deere & Company began tractor experiments in 1912, and finally built a hundred of the Dain All-Wheel-Drive tractors for the market in 1919. Yet, the Dain tractor was a moot design by the time the 1919 models were built; the previous year, Deere & Company bought out Waterloo Gasoline Engine Company of Waterloo, Iowa. This gained Deere the already established Waterloo Boy tractor, and put Deere genuinely into the tractor business within months.

Deere made improvements to the Waterloo Boy tractors and continued to market them until 1924. At that point the ubiquitous John Deere Model D tractor appeared. Through several different model changes, the Model D remained in production until 1953—nearly three decades of constant production.

I still recall the 1929 John Deere Model D we had on the farm. My dad bought it at an auction in 1946, then drove it about thirty miles back home. I don't recall exactly, but I know it was winter weather, and of course the ground was frozen. That should have been quite a trip, driving a steel-wheeled tractor for thirty miles on frozen ground! However, early in the spring, before fieldwork, the steel wheels made their last trip. I still recall my dad driving the old D to a local repair shop where the iron wheels were replaced with rubber tires.

During the winter months the D remained in the alley of the corn crib, belted to the hammer mill. Releasing the brake slacked the drive belt each time. In cold weather it took a pretty heavy shot of priming fuel, but virtually always, the D would start. Only once or twice can I remember carrying those buckets of hot water from the house out to fill the radiator and warm the cylinders a bit.

1958 John Deere Model 620 Orchard LPG
Owner: Verlan Hebrer. (Photograph © Ralph W. Sanders)

Finally about 1950, the D was traded on a styled John Deere Model G. The latter hadn't been in the field for long. However, it wouldn't perform very well, so in 1951 it was traded on a Massey-Harris Model 44 tractor. Later on, the next owner of the G did just as my dad had suggested; he put on a different magneto, and that cured the problems. Had the dealer at the time done that when my dad suggested it, my dad probably would have remained loyal to green and yellow.

Then of course there was the John Deere Gasoline Engine. When Deere bought out Waterloo Boy in 1918, it also inherited the latter's famous Waterloo Boy engine line. These continued on the market into 1923 when the famous E Series John Deere engines were introduced. Built in 1½-, 3-, and 6-horsepower sizes, these engines were built by the thousands. Among today's collectors they remain as one of the most sought-after of any engines, especially the 6-horsepower size.

For several years we had a small elevator with an attached 1½-horsepower John Deere engine. It leaked oil at various points, and this combined with oat hulls, corn dust, and other crib debris left it a rather sorry-looking sight. However, it would always start, and never caused any trouble.

When I first started collecting old engines in the

Man's Best Friend
A Farmer takes Rover for a ride on his Poppin' Johnny. (Minnesota Historical Society)

1950s, the first one I bought was a John Deere 6-horsepower model on factory trucks and with a belt pulley. The engine was in good shape except that it smoked badly. Then I found out that the plate between the crankcase and the fuel tank was rusted through, letting the oil drain down into the fuel tank. So, I traded it off on another engine, and that ended my career in the John Deere engine business. As time went on I developed my own likes and dislike in gas engines, and have specialized in diesel engines, oil engines, and rare examples of gasoline engines for more than thirty years now.

In our neighborhood there were many different makes of tractors. The John Deere was always popular, although in the 1940s and 1950s there were a lot of Oliver and IHC tractors. Massey-Harris gained a lot of popularity in the 1940s and 1950s, and there were a few Allis-Chalmers tractors, but very few from J. I. Case. Color loyalty seemed more important at the time, and many of those John Deere loyalists had bought green and yellow since the 1920s.

As times changed, so did the demographics. Some of the older dealers retired and went out of business. This happened with the Oliver line, and many of the Oliver folk switched over to John Deere. I recall the Deere folks bragging of how they could put in a new clutch without having to split the tractor—as was necessary for many of the other tractors—or they could completely dismantle the engine in a few hours.

To me, it seems incredible that the farm tractor saw the light of the world only a hundred years ago.

Trouble

A farmer labors to shovel out his John Deere Model D from a mudhole. (Glenbow Archives)

We began with huge, awkward, and clumsy machines suited mainly for belt work or plowing large areas of land. Now we have tractors that virtually have a brain, in that many of the engine and hydraulic activities are monitored electronically. We are able to chart activities via a GPS satellite, and have comforts within a tractor cab today that not even the most wealthy folk had thirty or forty years ago.

But then sometimes we long for those good old days. The old John Deere Model D had a three-bottom plow behind it. Going up a long grade provided stack music unlike anything we can recall . . . that throb of power at every impulse. I'm not so sure that stack music wouldn't be a welcome relief from the twang of guitars emanating from that modern, insulated tractor cab!

Tractors

By Bruce Bair

Entitled *Good Land, or, My Life as a Farm Boy*, Bruce Bair's memoir of growing up on his family's wheat farm near Goodland, Kansas, reads like a homegrown version of William Shakespeare's *King Lear*. The farm is the kingdom of Bair's father, Harold, a strong, stern, stubborn man who farmed with an inner fury as if he was waging war with fate.

Bair's memoir is not a romantic look book at the farm life, but by simply writing of the good and bad times on the farm, he exorcises demons and yet at the same time waxes nostalgic. Bair left the family farm to pursue a career as a writer and has worked on newspapers from Montana to South Dakota and back to his native Kansas. As he himself admits, there is something intangible that continually draws him back to the farm.

This chapter from *Good Land* tells of the glory of the John Deere Model D and a boy becoming a man.

1949 John Deere Model AW
Owner: Dennis Anderson. (Photograph © Andy Kraushaar)

If you want to bring a tear to an old farmer's eye, just show him a John Deere D. Despite the binders and threshers, steam tractors and Rumley OilPulls, which could run on anything from kerosene to old crankcase oil, Plains farming didn't take its present form until the advent of the John Deere D. With a D, a twelve-foot one-way and a long day, a farmer could turn under forty acres of stubble. Big farmers with lots of children could field platoons of Ds and farm almost anything for next to nothing. Ds were it.

Year after year, the D proved itself in the Nebraska Tractor Tests to be the most economical tractor. That is, you could farm more with less diesel fuel than by any other method. With the D came another invention, the combine. The combine is so called because it is a combination of a McCormick-Deering binder and a threshing machine. The first machines were awesome devices, pulled by teams of twelve or more horses. It wasn't long before inventors thought to put an internal combustion engine on the combine, and hook a D to it. Massey-Harris started making self-propelled combines. We were on our way.

Since these events occurred, dryland farming hasn't changed much. The tractors and combines have just gotten bigger, as have the farms, while the farmer's families have gotten smaller. And the farmers themselves have become almost as scarce as whitetailed jackrabbits.

Ds or tractors close enough to be called Ds were produced from the late thirties to the fifties. My father still thinks if you have one of those fifties Ds, why you have something. It has to be in good shape, though.

I was born in 1944, when my father was thirty years old. He'd gotten an exemption from military service because he was busy producing food for the world. He made a lot of money then and was busy plowing other fertile fields. My brother had been born three years earlier and my sister would come along about five years later.

Inexorable mathematics meant that by the time I turned eleven and weighed fifty-two pounds, I was ready. I was ripe. My father kept feeling my tiny, stringy biceps with his thumb and forefinger for a reason. Stupid me. I thought it was because he was proud of how strong I was getting. He thumped my head just like he thumped a watermelon to see if it were ripe. He put it in a head lock, to see how much pain I could stand.

And when my fifty-two-pound body had been built up enough by hauling two five-gallon pails of pig slop a furlong to the fence and filling up the water trough with twenty buckets of the same size from the tank an eighth-mile away, he deemed me ready.

1955. I was about to be jerked from my earthworks created by toy trucks and tiny tin tractors in the backyard into the real world of farming. I could be proud then, striding over the land in big boots with my chest stuck out.

He tried me out first when I was ten, on the Oliver 900. The 900 was a wonderful machine, built for pulling heavy loads, but not very versatile. Father used to have two of them. They were wonderful because instead of a single seat like most tractors had, they had a bench seat wide enough for three. In a pinch, the whole family could go for a tractor ride.

My father was stewing, crazy. He had to get something done. Even now I can remember how he was torn between fatherly responsibility (what if I got killed?) and the need to pull rod weeders over 160 acres of ground ahead of the drills. I'd been driving the 900 since I was eight, but never without supervision. He'd let me steer, which went fine until a corner needed turning. The front wheel of the 900 would catch in the one-way furrow and the wheel would spin back out of my control. If I didn't watch it, it would break my thumb. A big hairy forearm would reach over, slamming me back. Slamming me back in disgust—disgust that I just wouldn't grow fast enough to be useful or was so impossibly weak I couldn't wrestle an Oliver 900. He couldn't figure out why I had to be so small when Clark was so large. Hadn't Dr. Richardson, my birth doctor, measured the length at birth of my tibia and predicted I'd be tall?

But by and by, by nine, I'd take the tractor a round by myself, my pectorals straining.

My father couldn't stand it anymore. Labor

1934 John Deere Model A

Lester, Kenny, and Harland Layher pose with one of their many Poppin' Johnnies. (Photograph © Andy Kraushaar)

"Daddy's Little Helper"
Junior helps out Pa and the Johnny Pop-
per in this painting by Charles Freitag.
(Apple Creek Publishing)

unused. Labor playing with kittens. Labor dreaming in a bed on an afternoon with a black cat named Nancy. Labor stringing double lengths of garden hose all around the yard and rolling marbles down the crack. Labor chatting happily with its mother at dinner.

"Bruce is coming with me," he told my mother.

"What are you going to do with him?"

"I'm going to put his ass to work."

Who could have been happier? Who could have been prouder?

We drove to that rough quarter southeast of the "other place," fifteen miles from the dinner table, where I stood dwarfed by the Oliver 900.

"Get your ass up there."

I was like a puppy scrabbling over a gate.

Unlike the Rs we had then, the successors of the Ds, the Oliver ran quiet. Then as now, machinery was expensive. What we pulled were two iron-wheeled, thirties-era twelve-foot rod weeders. A rod weeder is simply a frame which holds a turning square rod about an inch in diameter. The rod is pulled just under the surface of the soil. Rod weeders are still in use. No finer machine has yet been invented to finish summer fallow prior to sowing. He didn't own a proper hitch, though. The weeders trailed behind a sweeps frame with the sweeps removed, one chain longer than the other.

He had that worried look about him. Forty years later, he still gets it whenever he thinks the work is getting behind. We only went a round or two together before he turned me loose. And around and around the field I went, alone, proud, doing a man's work at ten. Every hour or so, he'd come driving over the hill.

I'd stop.

"How you doing?"

I affected a drawl. I stood spraddle-legged in the dirt. I stuck my chest out. I was so stiff with pride I would have fallen except my lace-up farmer's boots wouldn't allow it.

"I guess I'm doing just fine." Nothing to it, Dad. It's easy.

He shook his head. I'll be damned, he seemed to be saying, the way he did when anything worth-less turned out to be worth something.

I'd get back on. Away I would go. The pickup would churn back through the dirt, over the hill.

I farmed and farmed, the field got smaller and smaller, the sun got closer and closer to the rim of the earth, and then the field was done. Only the corners were left. I was confident, an earth ripper, striding bigger than life over its face. He'd told me not to, but I wanted him to be proud. I decided to do the corners. What couldn't I do?

Off I went diagonally to the far corner of the field. I spun the wheel around confidently at the end. The tractor responded, turned back toward the center, and then lugged down for some reason. Frantically, I pressed the clutch, but not fast enough. A logchain link whizzed by my head like a thirty-thirty bullet. The tractor died. Behind, the two weeders had snarled together, the paddle wheels pulling them atop the sweeps. I had built a tower of twisted iron twenty feet tall. And I was in big trouble.

I had to walk over the hill. He saw me coming, trudging slump-shouldered, little puffs of dust following my bootheels, and I think he knew what was in store.

"What did you do? Try to do the corners?"

"Yes," I said.

"How bad is it?"

"It isn't too bad. Everything is all piled up is all."

I have never been able to figure out why atheists pray so much. He looked at the sky. "Jesus H. Christ," he said.

That ended tractor-driving that season. Everything worked out in the end. With the scoop tractor, the winch on the Power Wagon and the acetylene torch he and the hired hand got everything straightened out in about a day. I think my father even had a sense of backwards pride in me. No one in his memory had ever screwed up that big. And he admitted in whispers to Mother that I wasn't big enough and the whole deal was really his fault. He may have even told me that on the way home. In farming, if something needs doing, you take risks, even with the lives of small sons.

But why was I never told you could only turn that rig one way?

Mealtime
All work in the field comes to a halt when Ma and Sis arrive with the picnic lunch, as in this painting by Walter Haskell Hinton.
(Deere & Company)

Charles Freitag

A Farm Lad's Fantasy

By Orlan Skare

Orlan Skare was raised on a farm near Bagley, Minnesota, in the 1930s, earning his love for tractors and farming firsthand. He went on to serve as a traveling salesman for six years for Big Red—the International Harvester Company. He later became a professor of marketing and sales at the Willmar, Minnesota, technical college.

After he retired, Skare began putting down on paper recollections of his farming youth as a way to pass them on to his children and future generations. He has written of myriad memories, from the pain and suffering imposed by old-fashioned cast-iron tractor seats to the window that was opened to the world when radio arrived on the farm. His essays have appeared in Willmar's *West Central Tribune*.

Skare composed this collection of recollections in honor of the Johnny Popper.

"Snowman"
Farm children build the first snowman of winter with the help of their trusty Deere pedal tractor in this painting by Charles Freitag. (Apple Creek Publishing)

A farm lad operates a horse-drawn mower
Cutting a band of sweet-smelling hay
But he dreams of a time when horses are pastured
When power-farming offers a more promising way.

"Why buy gasoline for a tractor when you can raise oats and hay to fuel horses?" While Dad's reasoning made some sense in the cash-short early 1930s, it resulted in our farm being one of the last in the neighborhood to have a tractor.

The absence of a tractor on our farm only served to enhance my fascination for them. I had already decided that draft horses were sweaty, smelly, unpredictable beasts, interested in a young boy only if he was carrying a bucket of oats.

One of my early recollections is of a neighborhood thresherman turning into our farm driveway towing a threshing machine behind a steel-wheeled John Deere Model D. As he passed over a corner of Mom's well-tended garden to set his thresher between the round, tapered stacks of grain bundles, I recall thinking, "Mom's going to be angry about the rows of holes dug by the steel tractor cleats." I even tried to kick some of the clods of dirt back into the holes. Of course Mom wasn't angry; this was an acceptable reality of the times.

As the tractor operator was backing and turning his John Deere D to belt up to the thresher, I noticed him moving a long broomhandle-like lever back and forth. This didn't mean much to me at the time but I was later to learn that this was the infamous John Deere hand-clutch lever. The operator who had been standing while belting to the thresher had demonstrated a primary advantage of the hand clutch—its availability whether sitting or standing.

The John Deere D was considered a pretty big tractor at the time. I enjoyed watching the thresherman starting the engine. He first opened the petcock on each of the two, large cylinders in order to relieve some of the compression. After starting the engine by turning the large flywheel by hand, the engine made loud wheezing and spitting noises until the petcocks were closed.

Later in the 1930s, Dad and Mom gave serious thoughts to purchasing a small tractor that could be used both for haying and minor tillage work. International Harvester, Allis-Chalmers, and Ford-Ferguson had dealerships in Bagley. However, Dad and I favored the John Deere Model H, somewhat smaller than the more-popular Model B, but the closest John Deere dealer was in Fosston, Minnesota, twenty miles to the west of Bagley. How I dreamed about driving that little John Deere H!

But alas, we didn't act quickly enough and the outbreak of World War II killed our tractor-purchasing plans. We limped along during the wartime years with a "bug," a shortened Model A truck chassis that got us by quite well for haying, but was not very efficient for tillage purposes.

The two-cylinder design of early John Deere tractors provided a sound quite different from that of most other tractors. Wives of "Johnny Poppers" reportedly were able to determine when their husbands idled down the tractor for the trip home for lunch or dinner. This enabled them to have the food hot and on the table for the husband's arrival.

But there were other tractors with unique sounds. There were several Fordson tractors in our northern Minnesota neighborhood, and we could pinpoint their location a mile or two away by the transmission howl: "Sounds like Joe's working up his southwest forty this morning." Sometimes we could hear two or more Fordsons at the same time. Now bring in a farm dog with sensitivity to high-pitched sounds and you could have a howling country chorus!

The IHC Mogul and several other early tractors had one-cylinder engines that offered unique sounds of their own. These usually had heavy flywheels to smooth the engine's action, and many had governor-controlled intermittent firing and compression release. Someone claimed to be able to rapidly recite Abraham Lincoln's Gettysburg Address between the Mogul's firings while idling with no load. A dubious claim but the point is made.

Willmar, Minnesota, neighbor Irv Tallakson pointed out that the early Oliver 70 with six cylinders was especially smooth and quiet in operation, probably aided by the fact that Oliver was early in using full engine cowling.

1956 John Deere Model 420 Crawler
Owner: James Proctor. (Photograph © Ralph W. Sanders)

The steam-traction engines like those made by J. I. Case and Aultman & Taylor offered a paradox of sound. In spite of their huge size, they made little engine noise. These powerful engines were often almost inaudible when belted to a noisy threshing machine.

Finally, as a youngster I learned that there was a perverse way to create a sequential medley of sounds when pitching grain bundles into a threshing machine. I accidentally tossed a bundle crossways into the feeder. The threshing machine groaned as the bundle entered the cylinder, the tractor snorted loudly as the governor signaled to recover engine speed, and the thresherman bounded up cursing "What the heck are you doing, boy?" Definitely not a mistake to repeat again the same day.

Before the end of World War II, I was drafted into the Army, and upon discharge promptly entered college, got married, graduated, and began a job search. I still had tractor fantasies and my wife Beverly had some uncles who had fared well with International Harvester as company representatives. I brought a resume to the International Harvester district office then just a few blocks east of the University of Minnesota campus that I had attended.

1934–1938 John Deere Model As
Owners: Howard and Bonnie Miller.
(Photograph © Andy Kraushaar)

I began with IHC in March of 1950, worked for a short time in the office, before being transferred to a Wisconsin zone as a sales representative.

In the mid 1950s, a typical small Wisconsin town might have two or more full-line farm equipment dealers. IHC and John Deere were the most common, but Oliver, Case, Allis-Chalmers, Co-op, Ford, and others were also often represented.

As one part of my assistant zone manager assignment, I was to make farm calls with the dealer or a dealer's salesperson. The object was to get dealer personnel out to the farms, not simply waiting for customers to come through the front door.

These farm calls were fun and sometimes downright amusing. There was often lots of good-natured ribbing among John Deere and IHC owners.

"For Top Honors"

A John Deere Model A and a Farmall Model M face off against each other in a state fair tractor pull in this painting by Dave Barnhouse. (Artwork © Dave Barnhouse/Hadley Licensing)

Longtime John Deere owner Don Caine of Willmar recently reminded me of a couple of "tit for tat" quips:

Question: Why are John Deere tractors painted green?
Answer: So they can hide in the grass when a Farmall comes by.

Question: Why are Farmall tractors painted red?
Answer: So when the parts fall off they can be easily spotted in the grass.

I recall an IHC dealer salesman telling me partly in jest that he was willing to call on most farmers but hesitant to call on a John Deere owner. He further explained that in his experience, John Deere owners were so tired of being referred to as "Johnny Poppers" that they became downright irrational when someone proposed the four-cylinder engine used by IHC.

I'm now in retirement after teaching marketing for twenty-six years at Willmar Technical College (now Ridgewater College). I'm in reasonably good health except for minor bouts of DLD (acronym for Divided Loyalties Dilemma). For example, as I poke around my garage, I still wonder if there isn't some way that I could squeeze my childhood love, a John Deere H—or maybe a Farmall B temptress—into one of the garage corners. Now wait: If I were to put a canvas cover over my trailered boat and put it outside, maybe I could have one of each! Dilemma resolved.

1935 John Deere Model GP
Owner: Richard Bockwoldt. (Photograph © Andy Kraushaar)

CHAPTER 2

John Deere's Miraculous Mechanical Mule

"The infant gas tractor can stand the emergency endurance test where the horse and the mule fall down. He will pull all your tillage apparatus by moonlight as well as by daylight. If there is no moon all you have to do is to attach a searchlight."
—Barton W. Currie, *The Tractor*, 1916

T he first general-purpose tractors were really nothing more than mechanical mules, powered by gasoline rather than oats. From the 1920s on, as the gas tractors were refined, the days were numbered down on the farm for the flesh-and-blood mule and horse. The mechanical mule had won out with its iron-willed horsepower, and many a farmer bade a sad farewell to Old Dobbin as the horse was traded in on a Johnny Popper.

Turning the Soil
A farmer prepares the soil for planting on his John Deere Model A in the 1930s. (Photograph © J. C. Allen & Son)

JOHN DEERE
MODEL "D" TRACTOR

Outstanding Economy for all HEAVY FARM WORK

Sixty Years With a
John Deere Model D

By Bird J. Vincent

Bird J. Vincent lives on a centennial farm in Freeland, Michigan. He has written numerous articles chronicling life on his farm, from the old threshing days to memories of his favorite tried-and-true farm machines.

This article is a sort of timeline history of his family's John Deere Model D, chronicling every repair and modification made to the machine over the years as well as the nostalgic memories those simple repairs bring back.

1939 John Deere Model D Brochure

Our 1938 John Deere Model D, serial number 134761, was delivered in the spring of 1939. I was only five years old, but I can still remember the truck and trailer pulling into the driveway. The D had rubber front tires and steel lugs, and cost about $1,300.

That shiny new tractor was a great embarrassment to my late father a few days after in arrived. For some reason which even Mr. Thinker can't figure out, it was made with small, high-speed industrial sprockets on the drive axle. A neighbor, now in his late eighties, lived at the second farm north. He had an outbuilding on skids and wanted it moved. Dad went up with his big new D and hooked on to it. He couldn't move it. Another neighbor came and moved the building with an old Avery.

After Dad drove home, it didn't him long to get to the hand crank on the phone and ring up the dealer to come and fix the D. The dealer fixed the tractor on the wooden platform of a hay wagon scale we had in our front yard at that time. The transmission hasn't been worked on since except to change the gear oil.

The first tractor on our farm was a 1918 International Titan. I have pictures of it and a receipt for $1,557 dated November 8, 1918; the receipt includes the tractor and a John Deere three-bottom plow. The next tractor was an International 15/30. Then came the John Deere D, followed by a Ford 9N, Deere H, Deere A, Deere 3010, 4020, and 4250, and my son's Minneapolis-Moline ZB and Deere B pulling tractors.

Dad made a wooden toolbox that sits on the left side of the platform in front of the radiator shutter lever. It is painted International red. I spent many hours sitting on that toolbox when I was small. One

Building Muscles

A farmer puts his weight into spinning the flywheel to turn over the engine of his Deere. Starting one of the early Johnny Poppers was like taking the Charles Atlas Mr. Universe course. (Library of Congress)

1953 John Deere Model D
Owner: Mike Williams. (Photograph © Ralph W. Sanders)

"A Time of Plenty"
Fall brings a plentiful harvest in this painting by Dave Barnhouse. (Artwork © Dave Barnhouse/Hadley Licensing)

time, Dad was plowing and I looked down and saw the flywheel wobble. It was ready to come off. Dad stalled the D and fixed the problem. The flywheel still runs one-eighth inch beyond the crankshaft, but hasn't come loose in years.

When I was a little older, I would sit on the D as it powered the Case twenty-eight-inch thresher, Keck Gonnerman beaner, or Papec silo filler. I could operate the clutch and throttle when Dad would signal me by hand—a twirling hand above his head to speed up, hand up and down to slow, hand across the throat to stop. My four older brothers had to help with the heavy work like pitching bundles or carrying grain bags. Later, the two oldest went into the Army during World War II.

Dad threshed for about ten neighbors during the 1940s. When moving from farm to farm, he would drive the D and pull the thresher and one wagon. I would drive the 1941 Ford 9N, pulling two more wagons. My older brothers would drive the 1939 Mercury. Dad had canvas to cover the thresher, loaded wagons, and D at night. We carried planks to put down when we crossed the one tarvie road in the neighborhood.

I can still remember when I grew enough to be able to pull the flywheel and start the D. But it started hard when it was warm, so many times we would let it idle at meal times and only stop it to refuel.

It is still fun to watch a boy try to start it. You have to be strong enough to turn the flywheel and smart enough to let go when it fires. The sound of it starting is so pleasant that I look forward to it each spring and have even tape-recorded that sound for posterity.

Standard Oil made a special fuel for the John Deeres called "Power Fuel." When Standard stopped supplying Power Fuel, Dad put in a two-compartment overhead tank, with gasoline in one end and No. 1 fuel oil in the other. He would put both nozzles

1937 John Deere Model 62
Owner: Ron Jungmeyer. (Photograph © Ralph W. Sanders)

in the main tank and hold both open at the same time. It would start on gas, then switch and run on the blend. But you had to be sure the carburetor ran empty when it was shut down because it wouldn't start on the blended fuel.

We pulled an eight-foot double disc that would load up and be difficult to turn in sandy ground. Sometimes I had to unhook, back in on an angle, and hook up with a log chain we always had on the tractor. When the disc was turned sharp, it would unload. You would have to get it turned around and then rehook to the drawbar.

We still have the John Deere twelve-foot springtooth drag that was hooked from drawbar to the evener with a V-chain. One time, I turned too short, the chain caught the back tire, and came up and dented the fender before I could stop.

I used the D and drag last spring to incorporate one-third acre of oats for our threshing bee. I spread the oats with a Cyclone spreader on the Ford 9N. It's easier than getting the FBB drill out, and I like to have the D the first tractor working ground in the neighborhood each spring to show all the modern tractors the way.

The township had an Adams pull-type grader, the kind with the large hand wheels to set the depth at each end of the blade. I was driving and Dad was operating the grader, making a ditch. With every pass, the D was on more of a slant. Finally, it started to pound. Apparently it wasn't picking up oil. We decided the ditch was deep enough. (Mr. Thinker: Is the oil pickup off to one side?)

A dragline cleaned a large ditch on the south side of our farm and left the spoil in the field. To start to level it, we hooked up to a long barn beam with the D on one end and a neighbor's John Deere A on the other. The A was next to the ditch and would run a little ahead to give a grading action. But if the beam caught on a pile of dirt in the middle, I could keep moving and pull the A backward.

In 1947, the steel wheels were replaced with rubber tires. The man from the Firestone dealer came out and measured, took the wheels, cut the flat spokes off, and welded on thirty-inch rims and 15.5x30 tires (now 18.4x30). But he had measured

wrong and they would not fit under the fenders. He tried to get Dad to take the fenders off, but Dad refused. So the Firestone dealer cut the spokes again and installed twenty-eight-inch rims and the closed-tread Firestone tires loaded with CaC_{12} solution. The tire man lost his job because of the mistake.

The left rim split on the inside in about 1965. The tire rubbed and was ruined. I had a new rim welded on and replaced the tire with a Gates open-tread tire. The ends of the Gates tread bars would rub the flywheel when the D was turned and the tire flexed. You could smell the hot rubber. The flywheel wore a groove in the tire.

In 1995, we welded a patch on one rim, sand-blasted and painted the rims, and tried to install a new set of 18.4x28 Firestone tires. Again they were too large and rubbed. We put the old tires back on until we could get a set of 16.9x28 tires. We did not load these with CaC_{12}. This tire man did not lose his job because we knew it would be close, but I wanted the larger size if possible.

We also replaced the front tires with 7.50x18 Goodyear five-rib, like the ones that came on it. The pulley side had been replaced because it was cut so badly by the thresher drive belt. But the flywheel side was the original 1938 tire. It was weathered some on the outside, but the inside looked great yet.

One time a fan blade broke off in the field and was never found. Another time, the D had a magneto problem while threshing navy beans on our farm. We ran the Keck Gonnerman beaner with a neighbor's Farmall M that day.

The D's engine was first overhauled at Rogers John Deere in LaPorte, Michigan. I can remember seeing it with the head off and seeing how large the piston bore was. My older brother, Jim, can remember the bill for a simple ring and valve grind was forty-five dollars.

The next—and last—overhaul was done at Dad's brother's Ford dealership in Auburn, Michigan. This time, the block was removed and bored oversize. At the same time, a large Fram oil filter was installed just behind the gas tank. Fram no longer makes a replacement filter so it hasn't been changed for about

Threshing Time

A rubber-tire-equipped John Deere Model D runs a threshing machine in 1936. (Photograph © J. C. Allen & Son)

thirty years. It still gets warm, so oil must flow through it.

We kept a spare magneto on hand for the D. It does not have the original on it now. A few years ago, we had the magneto and carburetor rebuilt. It runs great yet.

The steering got loose and we rebuilt it. A local machine shop made a new pin and bushing for where the wishbone attaches to the crankcase. We found out the hard way that the engine oil drains when you remove that pin. The crank arm at the bottom of the vertical steering shaft is welded to the shaft because the tapered splines are worn. This was a problem over the years. The tie rod ends and the bolts that hold the steering gear box were tightened. The steering is good now.

The D was stripped, primed, and painted in 1985. The hood is rusted near the radiator from water sloshing out, and the top of the exhaust pipe has eroded away.

A few years ago, we found and purchased the same Co-op plow that the D used to pull. It had been sold twice. The third bottom has been removed, but two fourteens are enough to bring back the memories and my son can also pull it with his Deere B.

We have a threshing bee on our centennial farm every year, and operate the binders, threshers, and the silo filler with that old D. The fourth generation is now operating the D, and it should last for a good many more years to come.

War, Peace, and Tractors

By Colleen McCarty-Gould

Colleen McCarty-Gould of Rosemont, Minnesota, is the author of several humorous essays on the world of John Deere and old tractor collectors. She is also the author of an important and considered book entitled *Crisis and Chaos: Life With the Combat Veteran: The Stories of Families Living and Coping With Post-Traumatic Stress Disorder.*

In this autobiographical essay, she combines her two writing fields of knowledge into a touching story of her husband and herself coping with Post-Traumatic Stress Disorder and the healing powers of a John Deere tractor.

1949 John Deere Model BW
Owner: Dennis Anderson. (Photograph © Andy Kraushaar)

The years had been hard since his return from Vietnam. The nightmares, the flashbacks, the memories of fallen comrades. Nothing seemed right since he stepped off that plane and landed back home in September of 1972.

He was not quite twenty-one, but the stress of battle had turned him into an old man. I didn't know him then; our chance meeting wouldn't happen for a couple of years yet. But family and friends who had grown up with him say that those experiences in a faraway place had changed him forever.

I met Dale in 1974, a couple of years after his return. He had landed a job, bought a car, and seemingly settled back into civilian life. To those around him, he appeared eager to catch up on the lost years; he talked often about buying a home, meeting someone, and getting married. He frequently compared himself to friends who had taken the usual route in life rather than the ragged path of war.

We married in 1986 and set up house immediately. At first, life was routine and uneventful. We went about the business of marriage: working, paying bills, and enjoying an occasional night out. We even bought a dog to cement Dale's vision of what civilian life was supposed to be like. We dreamt of a quiet, fulfilling future, the kind that our parents and their parents before them had enjoyed.

But Vietnam was never far behind us. Though Dale tried hard to forget those eighteen months in that faraway place, he simply could not. He remembered the big things—the sound of mortar shells and the sight of powerful helicopters that dotted the blue skies. And he remembered the little things—the heat and smell of the jungle and the last breath of a dying friend.

For the next ten years, we battled the ghost of Vietnam together. The days were dark and lonely and filled with the kinds of nightmares that only a glimpse at hell could bring. Dale's behavior became more and more erratic as he succumbed to the stranglehold of Post-Traumatic Stress Disorder (PTSD), a disorder common in combat veterans of all ages and from all wars. Eventually, the government gave Dale a 100 percent disability rating, and

we resigned ourselves to a life of sadness and uncertainty.

Indeed, war hung on as Dale continued to grapple with his past. The symptoms and behaviors of PTSD played funny tricks on us, seeming to come and go at will. The years blurred in a constant round of hospitalizations, medications, and feelings of hopelessness. The only time either of us stopped long enough to catch our breath was to wonder when and where the craziness would end.

It came on a warm, late-fall Sunday in 1996. The moment when I first remember thinking that maybe things could get better. Dale and I were taking a leisurely drive, not far from our suburban home outside St. Paul, Minnesota. The drive was nice; we had just enjoyed lunch and were engaged in casual chatter, the kind with no particular importance or purpose. We relished in the ease of the day, for such comfortable times had become scarce in our lives.

Dale was the first to spot the for-sale sign. It came so quickly, as we rounded the bend of that busy highway. There it was, off to the lefthand side of the road. "For sale." Nothing more than that. But there didn't have to be; the house we had driven by and admired so many times before was up for grabs on that particular day. The big, yellow house surrounded by acres and acres of land.

I watched Dale as we drove up the driveway to the big, yellow house. It was the first time in years that I had seen in him a spark of excitement. He spoke in short, choppy sentences and he breathed hard. "We've got to call someone. I've got to have this house. You don't understand. It's important for me to have this house."

He got out of the car and approached the front door. He knocked, but no one answered. Then he walked around to the back and stared at the long, deep yard and wildlife pond at the end of the property. He stood there, seemingly lost in thoughts of some other time and place. I nudged and reminded him that we were trespassing and that maybe we had better make an appointment before examining things so closely. But Dale didn't care. I knew he was home.

Unstyled and Styled John Deere Model BWH-40s

Owners: Walter and Bruce Keller. (Photograph © Andy Kraushaar)

The weeks and months that followed were consumed with buying the big, yellow house and the acreage it stood on. We faced a lot of adversity in closing the deal—mainly the fact that the property was too expensive for us. But we held on to the vision of owning that house and the land and all that it meant for us. In May of 1997, we took possession.

The day was very much like that warm, fall day when we first spotted the house. Sunny and hopeful. We drove up the long driveway and Dale leaped out before I could park the car. Keys in hand, he opened the door to his new, old house and walked in. I came in shortly after him and we both stood and stared at the empty room before us. We marveled at being the new owners.

"Dale, what is it about this place that makes you so happy?" I couldn't help but ask.

Besides the large size of the house and the endless yard, it was after all merely a house and we had owned a nice house. I couldn't quite grasp what brought him such joy.

He turned to me and said softly, "It reminds me of times before the war, like when I was a kid. It's an old-fashioned house, the kind that my grandmother lived in. It makes me feel peaceful and good. It makes me forget."

In my heart, I had already figured it out. The

big, yellow house did indeed look like something out of an old oil painting. Not a grand house, not even a well-cared-for house. It had plenty of flaws; I could tell immediately that life here was going to involve lots and lots of work. But I didn't care. If Dale could find peace, then I could find peace there, too.

We settled in and adjusted to caring for a large, old home and ten acres of land. I quickly discovered that Dale's peace came with a huge pricetag. My days were overly committed; I added all the responsibilities of taking care of the interior of the home to working a full-time, professional job. At the end of each long day, I collapsed, exhausted.

Dale worked just as hard in caring for the land and the outside of the house. The endless chores worked wonders on his mind; he simply had no time to remember the traumas of war. With each passing day, the memories faded just a little bit more.

Yes, life with Dale was becoming what I had always hoped it would be. Though the days were tough in their own way, they were actually easier; there were no surprises, no quick trips to the hospital, or crazy behavior to deal with. I felt that, for the first time in our marriage, Dale and I were on a common path and working toward a common goal.

And then, about two months into our new routines, Dale announced that he had some important things to say about the situation, about our new lives in the big, yellow house. My heart fluttered; I wondered what lay in store for me and my tired, old soldier.

At first he hedged. Then he planted himself directly in front of me, took a deep breath and blurted: "My part of the deal is a lot harder than yours. It's a lot tougher taking care of ten acres than taking care of the inside of the house. I need a John Deere tractor. And I need one now."

I relaxed. That was it? Dale's big announcement? How wonderful! I had imagined the worst. I had imagined all sorts of bad things—things that would certainly disrupt the lives we were now creating.

1936 John Deere Model BO
Owner: Bruce Wilhelm. (Photograph © Ralph W. Sanders)

66

"Pitching In"
Junior pitches in with his Deere pedal tractor in this painting by artist Donald Zolan. (Artwork © Zolan Fine Arts, LLC. Ridgefield, CT)

68

Above:
1930s John Deere Model AO
Owner: Irv Baker. (Photograph by Hans Halberstadt)

Left:
1949 John Deere Model AW
Owner: Dennis Anderson. (Photograph © Andy Kraushaar)

1951 John Deere Model R
Owner: Chad Reeter. (Photograph © Ralph W. Sanders)

"Of course you need a John Deere!" I was only too thrilled to agree with him. In fact, I would have bought Dale a John Deere that very second if I had known where to find one. But I didn't. I actually didn't know anything about John Deere except that it was going to save my life and my marriage. And, more importantly, it was going to make Dale very happy.

We set about finding just the right John Deere. Not too big, but not too small, either. It had to handle our ten acres with ease—both summer cutting and winter plowing. Dale made it a mission to study all the John Deeres out there; I let him be the general on this one as I was definitely the private when it came to tractors. And anyway, I was only too pleased that he was excited about something. There had been no talk of war and Vietnam in a long time.

Dale eventually selected his John Deere, a large riding lawn mower—the next step to a full-sized tractor, he explained. Then he anxiously awaited the day of delivery.

Delivery day was grand indeed! Dale gathered me and a couple of friends and family to await the arrival. He had already made special preparations by clearing out a spot in the garage—relegating my car to a lesser spot—and buying an assortment of accessories and trinkets. When it finally arrived, Dale instructed all of us to step aside and make room for the newest addition to the family. He also announced the obvious—that no one (including me) was to ever touch or drive his John Deere. Not ever.

Dale quickly adapted to driving the mower. Overnight, it became his prized possession. And in conversations that could easily have included war and Vietnam, there was none. Instead, there was talk of Model Bs and Gs and all sorts of green-and-yellow chitchat. References to Vietnam all but disappeared.

In fact, weeks passed with no mention of war and killing. Dale made new friends, John Deere friends who collect and restore and talk of nothing but tractors. I relished in my husband's new obsession; it made life normal and fun again. It also bonded us, as I began to develop an interest in tractors, too.

We even bought John Deere toys and decorated a part of the house in a John Deere theme.

As with all things in life, though, our new-found interest came with a pricetag. Dale soon discovered that one tractor did not a collection make. He set out on a mission to get another John Deere, this time an old tractor. He threw out terms like "Two Cylinder" and "New Generation." All I really understood was that such talk meant dollars and an impact on our family budget.

But I didn't care. I was much too content with our new lives in the big, yellow house—even if it did mean filling it up with green-and-yellow machinery.

Dale added an old 1944 Model B to his collection of two. It's "a real beauty," he says. The parts are vintage, the paint is fresh, and the overall look is perfect. Having been around Dale's obsession long enough, I was only too happy to agree with him. He also announced his intention to be on the lookout for many more tractors.

Through the years, Dale has kept his Vietnam vet friends along with his new John Deere friends. The vets are respectful of Dale's new joy and often joke about him being a member of that "John Deere unit." For his fiftieth birthday party, he enjoyed a wonderful mixture of friends from all of his special relationships.

Dale's joy appears to be long-lasting and deep. He frequently comments on the amazing change in his life. He often credits his tractors for their calming influence and he sighs: "I love to sit out in my garage and just listen to the engine. There's nothing quite like it in the world."

I, in the meantime, am convinced that life has taken a pleasant turn. I savor the simple moments—like seeing Dale on his tractor, at dawn or dusk, on a warm summer day. His silhouette is so still. I can't make out his face, but I am assured that it is content. He cuts the grass so precisely, so evenly, that it is obvious he is executing a plan and carrying out a mission.

But unlike those missions of so long ago, this one will end victoriously. For once, Dale is at peace—with himself and the world.

Above:
1952 John Deere Model AH Hi-Crop
Owner: Lloyd Sheffler. (Photograph © Andy Kraushaar)

Right:
1950s John Deere Model 620 Orchard.
Owners: Jim, Kraig, and Kurt Wileman. (Photograph © Andy Kraushaar)

CHAPTER 3

History and Heritage of the Modern John Deere

"Although we did not realize it at the time, the first indication of the momentous news to come was the 1959 announcement of the 215-hp articulated 8010 tractor and its eight-bottom integral plow at the vast Marshalltown, Iowa, show. No one outside of Deere's inner circle knew what this announcement portended, but it signaled the end of the two-cylinder era. . . ."
—Don Macmillan, *The Big Book of John Deere Tractors*

With the arrival of the New Generation of Power tractors in 1960, John Deere entered a new era in its history. Gone were the old two-cylinder Johnny Poppers, replaced by four- and six-cylinder modern machines. To some, it was sad news. To others, it was a necessary step forward into the future of agriculture, and those New Generation machines became the forerunners of the John Deere tractors still being built today.

1965 John Deere Model 4020
Owner: Tom Manning. (Photograph © Ralph W. Sanders)

The New Generation: Revolutionary, Not Just Evolutionary

By Chester Peterson Jr.

Chester "Chet" Peterson Jr. has been involved in farming since his 4-H days in Kansas. He later served as an editor at *Successful Farming* magazine, started and published *Kansas Business News*, and was the publisher of *Simmental Shield*. Chet is now a full-time freelance writer and photographer specializing in agriculture. He is also the author of several tractor histories, including *Vintage Allis-Chalmers Tractors*, published by Voyageur Press.

In this essay, he chronicles the startling arrival of the New Generation of Power and the wide-reaching effects it had on John Deere and farming as whole.

1961 John Deere 3010 and 4010
Owner: Ken Smith. (Photograph by Hans Halberstadt)

It was a surprise that no one expected. John Deere's modernized line of "New Generation of Power" tractors was introduced with great fanfare on August 30, 1960, in Dallas, Texas, and startled the whole agriculture industry. These new tractors were not merely evolutionary upgrades but revolutionary in their very nature.

They not only replaced the venerable and beloved two-cylinder "Johnny Putt-Putts," but also set amazingly high—and at the time virtually unreachable—standards for the rest of the agricultural-equipment industry.

In that one day, New Generation of Power tractors changed the image of Deere & Company. No longer was Deere an industry follower and perennial number two to International Harvester. Now, Deere was suddenly a pace-setter.

There was no magic wand waved to instantly produce these four- and six-cylinder tractors. Instead, they were the result of a seven-year-long gestation that began when then President and CEO Charles Wiman decided—allegedly without consulting the board of directors—to start the development process.

For much of this research and development period, though, the chief motivator was his successor and son-in-law, Bill Hewitt. Convinced the time was right for a change, Hewitt started with a blank sheet of paper. He also was aware that the new line's extensive research and development would have to be maintained in strictest secrecy. Naturally, he didn't want to alert the competition. Maybe even more important, he emphasized that the company could ill-afford to lose sales if word got out that a new tractor was being designed to obsolete the present popular models.

The result was secrecy that rivaled the Manhattan Project of World War II that produced the atomic bomb. People assigned to the development project worked on it exclusively. And, for the first few months, they did it in an unlikely facility removed from the usual company environment. An unused grocery store in downtown Waterloo, Iowa, nicknamed the "meat market," served as the initial

engineering center in 1953. Three years later, Deere's state-of-the-art Project Engineering Center was completed.

Only a selected few in the entire company knew what was going on. More than one mid- to high-level executive failed to gain entrance due to a lack of proper credentials.

There were several "givens" for the engineers and designers: The new tractor had to be able to utilize the same mounted equipment as the present line. And stress was placed on one person being able to hook up and detach implements.

Although V-engines of four, six, and eight cylinders as well as a horizontal four were studied in Model "A" testbeds, all had various shortcomings. Many transmissions were also studied and discarded.

An important aspect of engine design is determining the center-line dimensions of the block in order to locate the cylinders. Deere did its job right here, and is still utilizing the same fixed cylinder center dimensions of the New Generation tractors in its engines today.

A totally new transmission was needed for some of the tractors, the 3010 and 4010. Such design was still being done then in the industry via drawing board and hand calculations were done to eight decimal places.

Equally pushed for both time and required accuracy, one Waterloo engineer wrote the first computer program for computer-aided gear design. Even though the computer—located a three-hour drive away at the Moline, Illinois, company headquarters—was of the punch-card type, what it spit out in fifteen minutes of work equaled up to eight hours of handwork. Oh, yes, and the computer design allowed a gearset that safely delivered 20 percent more power through the gears.

Excessive gear noise while under load plagued 1010 and 1020 prototypes. No solution worked, and show-and-tell time was fast approaching. Finally, one engineer suggested changing the straight-cut gears to helical. When the new gears were assembled, darkness had fallen. No matter. The tractor was

1960 Deere 8010

Owners: Walter and Bruce Keller. (Photograph by Chester Peterson Jr.)

"Bumper Crop"
Old and new generations of Deere trac-
tors work together to bring in the har-
vest in this painting by Charles Freitag.
(Apple Creek Publishing)

quietly driven to the adjacent test plot. And, then while under load, it continued at what one engineer described as "whisper quiet."

However, probably the greatest mechanical achievement of the New Generation tractors was the hydraulic system. To put this into perspective, remember that all other conventional gear pumps of this period could only maintain 1,000 psi. The new eight-piston pump delivered 20 gallons a minute at 2,000 psi.

Power on demand to power steering, brakes, three-point hitch, and remote cylinders was provided by the closed-center system. When not in use, this power system demanded only a 1.5 horsepower drain from the engine.

There's also a good reason why the PTO control lever on the new line of tractors was located to the right side of the console—well, a reason anyhow. After checking out the seat of a prototype, a well-placed company "suit" rose, then pivoted left to exit the platform. The hem of his coat caught the PTO lever, and a new, ragged coat vent resulted. Almost immediately a suggestion came down from higher up to relocate the PTO lever to the console's right.

Secrecy prevailed while prototype test models moved to and from field test facilities. More often than not these tractors were painted red and carried various additions to camouflage the new sheet-metal design.

It wasn't so easy to disguise the sound of the new four- and six-cylinder engines, since their exhaust certainly wasn't the familiar two-cylinder beat. Apparently, however, no industrial spies were listening outside the Project Engineering Center building where engine tests were run.

Naturally, it was impossible for Deere & Company to produce all the parts necessary to construct prototypes and production tractors. To prevent tipping anyone off, the purchasing staff was instructed to order outsourced parts from as many suppliers as possible.

For the first time in the industry, the tractor's sheet metal was designed to appeal to women as well as men. Deere has always been known for keeping tabs on the pulse of the market. It learned that more and more farm wives were accompanying their husbands to dealers and being part of the buying decision.

A longtime design consultant for Deere & company, Henry Dreyfuss, tackled the problem of combining styling with operator comfort and convenience. His philosophy was that if two competing makes of tractors were comparable in performance, price, and dealer service, then the buying decision became largely a function of styling

In a way, design of the New Generation tractors was like an awakening from the Dark Ages. For instance, up until this time, seat design was rather simple. "Ol' Sam," considered to have the biggest fanny in the Waterloo plant, was asked to sit in plaster of Paris. From this cast, the seat was shaped. The thought was that if Ol' Sam could fit it, well, then just about everyone else would, too.

Believing there had to be a better way and wanting the most comfortable seat ever made for these new tractors, Dreyfuss brought in a human posture specialist named Dr. Janet Travell. This lady doctor watched tractors being operated over various types of terrain by drivers weighing 110 to more than 220 pounds. She then came up with a seat backrest that was in two levels, new armrests with just the right amount of firmness, and a much better designed seat that was firmer under the pelvic bones and softer under the driver's thighs.

Probably the best thing she did was point out the need for a seat that was spring-loaded instead of being attached rigidly to the tractor. Seat travel was limited to a maximum of four inches.

Her next best move was suggesting the addition of a lever so the driver could adjust the seat spring's tension to match his or her weight and preference. This was also an innovation at the time.

Quite soon what was offered as a $50 deluxe seat option proved so popular that it was made standard equipment.

The lady doctor became even more famous the year after the new line of tractors was introduced: In early 1961, Dr. Travell was appointed the White House physician by new President John F. Kennedy.

* * *

1961 John Deere 3010 and 4010
These are the first 3010 and 4010 tractors made. Owner: Ken Smith. (Photograph © Ralph W. Sanders)

What Deere & Company did during this era to safe-guard tractor drivers has both saved lives and influenced the entire industry. The stimulus for this was a Deere test tractor mounting a loader that rolled over and killed its driver while making turn tests at night.

The first thought of the engineers was to provide protection for company test drivers. This was quickly followed by the logical thought that farmers have an equal need for a safety roll cage.

Since nobody knew anything about what was needed, the engineers bought a mannequin for use during a complex testing program. After testing many different designs, at one point they thought they had the answer. They weren't quite there yet, however.

Somewhere in Deere's archives allegedly there's a movie of this design's final test. The remote-controlled tractor with a mannequin in the driver's seat starts up a steep incline. An engineer pulls the rope that makes it tip over—then is seen throwing his hat to the ground as the roll cage shatters. Back to the drawing board.

After completing its roll-guard work, Deere

1960 John Deere 8020
Owners: Mike and Rick Hoffman. (Photograph by Chester Peterson Jr.)

invited all it competitors to view it in operation. It then generously offered to not only provide these companies with the design and materials specifications, but also to help them with any manufacturing problems.

It was an easy step from thinking about roll guards to cabs. Three ideas guided cab design. First, it was to be like a car body in that it couldn't be converted. Second, it must be unlike all the other tractor cabs being produced that were excessively noisy. Third, it had to be comfortable for a driver who might be working in it for twelve to fourteen hours a day.

Lacking experience in this area, the engineers contacted colleagues they knew who worked for the Big Three automobile companies. They also hired an acoustical engineer consultant.

In this way, the fast-stepping Chevrolet Corvette and the John Deere cab almost became cousins. A. O. Smith, the company that made the Corvette bodies for Chevrolet, was slated to get the Deere manufacturing contract. However, Deere executives decided the profit potential was greater if the cab was produced inhouse.

How good was this first cab, which has now evolved into the Sound-Gard cab? An early model was on a tractor being hauled by a semi-truck when the entire unit overturned in a ditch. Although no longer looking like new, the cab still was stout enough to hold up the combined weight of the tractor and semi-trailer.

The innovative cab was easily the quietest, most dust-free, quietest cab ever to ride a tractor. Noise level was akin to the interior of an automobile, thanks to four rubber biscuits that insulated it from noise transmitted through the tractor's frame and other engineering tweaks.

In fact, there was only one little problem with it when marketed: Phone calls started coming in from all over the world wondering what the engineers had done to make the cab so blasted uncomfortable, and demanding a fix.

Huh? Another consultant, an industrial psychologist, located the problem. He began by explaining that at the General Motors test track its engineers had a specially rigged car. A dial on the dashboard was pointed out to a driver as something that would control the comfort of his ride. The driver then assumed that the dial had something to do with adjusting the car's suspension or his seat or both.

Wrong. The dial had nothing to do with either. Instead, it subtly controlled the interior noise level. Just about every driver wheeled back in with the dial set for a noise level on the higher end of the scale. Yet he was more comfortable.

The scientific answer is that our hearing process is both complex and demanding of our attention. In simple terms, the louder an environment is, the less our brain listens to the nerve endings in our posteriors. Think of this as a classic case of overload.

So, in this case, the Deere & Company engineers had outdone themselves. They'd made their new Sound-Gard cab so quiet that even the slightest vibration in the seat area now received attention. Before, nobody really noticed it even when the seats were uncushioned metal. At this point, the engineers considered undoing some of their improvements in order to allow the new cab to be somewhat noisier, and so more "comfortable." In the end, though, they decided to make no changes and simply let the operators get used to the different setup.

There was one error made concerning these new cabs, though. Original estimates were that only 15 percent of the buyers would order cabs. The actual initial figure was closer to 50 percent, and soon increased to 75 percent.

Due to all its glass, a tractor cab generally requires twice the air conditioning as an automobile. At the time, all the other aftermarket cabs utilized a reciprocating piston-type compressor. It was ugly, set up too high on the engine, and didn't provide that great a cooling job.

Deere & Company engineers thought General Motors made the best air-conditioning unit. But big GM said they didn't sell to outside manufacturers.

But where there's a will, there's a way: One of the top Deere engineers was on a Society of Automotive Engineers committee with a factory

1969 John Deere 4020
Owner: Herb Altenburg. (Photograph © Andy Kraushaar)

manager at Frigidaire, a GM company. This man didn't want to sell his compressors either. His main apprehension was that the units would somehow be changed, and so might sully the Frigidaire name if word got out if problems arose. The Deere engineer finally convinced the Frigidaire executive to sell compressors for use with the new cabs for New Generation tractors. However, he had to promise that they'd be used as is without any changes.

The compressors worked just great on test tractors—for 200 hours or so. Then the dust of fieldwork and vibration beyond that of automobile highway usage started the seals leaking.

In a process that ate up two and a half years of development time, Deere engineers came up with a new bearing and dust and vibration boxes for the compressors. Then the company supplying the seals to GM was contacted and asked to come up with modified seals, but not to inform GM, of course.

The revamped unit fit the same space. More important it worked and worked and worked, regardless of the harshness of the conditions in which the tractor was working.

Then and only then did the lead Deere engineer tell the Frigidaire people that the promise not to change anything had been slightly bent. But, not to worry, the modified compressor now worked so much better and the cost was the same. And, according to Deere & Company lore, the compressor of every air-conditioned GM car to this day contains the modifications that first appeared on John Deere New Generation tractors.

Production tractors have to have model designations. Most previous John Deere tractors had carried letters, such as the Models A, D, and R, with little logic used in selection. A completely new-from-the-soil-up tractor deserved an equally new method of nomenclature, executives agreed.

Why 2010 or 3010? Why, in other words, four numbers rather than fewer numbers or letters?

The answer is that four numerals can easily be voiced in two catchy words: "Twenty-ten" and "Thirty-ten," for example. This also made later improved models both easy to name while retaining familiarity by substituting "Twenty-twenty" and "Thirty-twenty."

Another continuing benefit of the New Generation concept was the implementation of the "world-wide" concept for the company. Depending on the country in which it was built, each tractor of the same model up until 1962 was somewhat different.

All drawings after that date presented specifications also in metric numbers. Symbols replaced many drawing notes, too. The payoff was that for the first time any Deere & Company factory in the world could then work from the same drawings.

It would be difficult to keep a secret if you threw a party for 6,500 people from twenty countries, rolled in 136 new tractors and 223 pieces of equipment, arranged for vast quantities of food, lined up entertainment, located housing in twenty-one hotels, rented 100 charter buses, and coordinated flights on sixteen airlines plus charters. Yet that's what Deere & Company did. The New Generation tractor veiled in secrecy for its entire development life was released to the complete surprise of dealers, journalists, industry leaders, and yes, even to some company executives on August 30, 1960, in Dallas, Texas.

The event itself required two years of planning and preparation, the work of hundreds of employees, and even a specially designed miniature of the Memorial Auditorium.

Since Dallas was the home of the famed Neiman-Marcus department stores, it seemed only proper that the new star of the agricultural tractor industry should be on display there. All during "D-Day," a new 3010 tractor was on exhibition at Neiman-Marcus. It was gussied up with a diamond bracelet at the top of its exhaust stack and the "John Deere" logo on both sides of the hood was spelled out with diamonds. The value of the diamonds was estimated at $2 million.

There's a tale about that particular tractor. One of the Deere people tasked with getting the new tractor into and then back out of the store soon learned that it wouldn't fit through the doors. So, he and his crew had to take out a display window the night before in order to get the tractor into the store.

Then somebody noticed that its metal tag on the rear housing was blank where the serial number should have been. Thinking the space should be filled, he hammered in a "0." Years later, Deere received a call from a Nebraska farmer requesting information about an usual 3010 he was restoring. The caller said, "Kind of funny. But the only serial number this tractor carries is a zero."

It could be justifiably argued that regardless of a long history of innovation over the years, the real turning point in Deere & Company's history took place 131 years after John Deere set up his first blacksmith shop. The New Generation tractors helped establish Deere on the road to dominance in the farm-equipment industry. The company even recently reported an annual net profit of more than a billion dollars.

A "windshield survey" readily provides evidence concerning the popularity of tractors wearing the familiar green and yellow. All owe much to their forerunner, the New Generation tractor that changed so much in the industry.

And, heck, a lot of these sturdy New Generation tractors are still doing a steady day's work four decades after they went out the factory door.

1960s John Deere 4000 Diesel
Owners: Jim, Kraig, and Kurt Wileman. (Photograph © Andy Kraushaar)

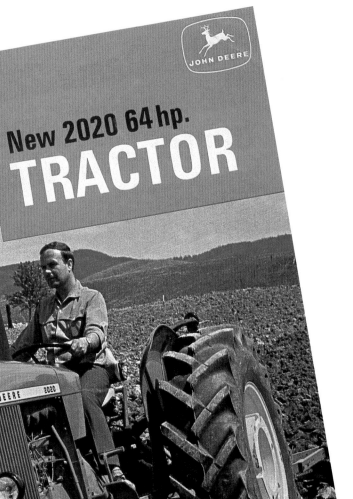

New 2020 64 hp.
TRACTOR

JOHN DEERE

The Saga of the New Generation Prototype Tractors

By Ralph Hughes

Ralph Hughes joined Deere & Company in 1954 as a writer for the company's magazine *The Furrow*. Through the years at Deere, he became an advertising copywriter and, eventually, the Director of Advertising.

Ralph is the author of numerous articles and books on Deere, including the company's own history *How Johnny Popper Replaced the Horse*, a glorious look back at the first Deere tractors. Since his retirement from Deere, Ralph has continued to write about the company in numerous publications, including *John Deere Tradition* magazine.

In this essay, Ralph tells the inside story of life as a Deere advertising man assigned to promote the then-new 1020 and 2020 tractors.

Shortly after the John Deere "New Generation of Power" tractors were introduced in Dallas and deliveries began to farmers, reports from dealers and letters from customers came back to Deere & Company. The Waterloo-built 3010 and 4010 tractors were a big success; farmers loved them. The Dubuque-manufactured 1010 and 2010 tractors, however, fell short of expectations.

The less-than-favorable reports on the 1010 and 2010 may not have been a complete surprise to Deere's management and factory engineers. They were aware that the introductory timetable for the "New Generation of Power" tractors didn't provide as much engineering and testing time for the two smaller tractors as it did for their larger-horsepower counterparts.

Whether or not it was a fact, a few critics even suggested that the new 1010 was basically a "warmed over" Model 430 tractor with a variable-speed four-cylinder engine and new sheet metal. Such a comment was not made regarding the 2010 tractor, because it was styled more closely to match the Waterloo models. It was basically a small version of the 3010 with the same type of fenders, deluxe seat, and dashboard-mounted controls. Unfortunately, the 2010 lacked the reliability built into its Waterloo brothers. Another frequent criticism was that the 1010 and 2010 did not have all of the convenience features provided on the new 3010 and 4010.

Deere's response to these reports was the introduction in 1965 of two totally new tractors, the 1020 and 2020. That' was the year my personal adventure with the 1020 and 2020 began—not as an engineer, but as an advertising copywriter. During the next twelve months, I not only helped to create the promotional materials for these two new tractors, but also became a mechanic with skinned knuckles and a black-and-blue toe. I learned to become an early-to-rise, late-to-bed railroader; an art buyer; a part-time motion-picture grip; and finally, a well-traveled interviewer.

Now is a good time to clear up a misunderstanding some readers may have regarding how farm tractor advertising was prepared thirty-five years ago.

First of all, there was usually a shortage of prototype tractors. Prototypes are costly to build because they are handmade; only a minimum number are produced. First of all, prototype tractors are sent to test farms for field trials. Then, the factories that manufacture matched working equipment for John Deere tractors need prototype tractors to make sure the attachments they produce fit properly. For example, a front loader has to be mounted and hooked up hydraulically to make sure it attaches as easily as it should and has the clearances required for raising and lowering. The same is true with a front-mounted, row-crop cultivator. Even though there should be no problem with three-point-hitch-mounted equipment, each attachment must be tested to determine how much, if any, additional front weight may be needed on the tractor. During this fitting process, photographs of the attachments are taken on the prototype tractors for the operator manuals that are needed prior to the introduction of the new tractors.

Often, the advertising copywriter is the low man on the totem pole, the last to be provided a prototype tractor for photographic purposes. Several photographs were needed for new sales literature and for print ads to run in *The Furrow* and other farm publications. Motion-picture footage was also required for introductory meetings and dealer Farming Frontiers shows.

Rarely are there sufficient prototype tractors available to fill all of the requirements. Such was the situation in 1965, when I was assigned to create advertising materials for the new John Deere 1020 and 2020 tractors. To compound the problem, six, not two, prototypes were needed, because the new 1020 and 2020 tractors were each to be offered in three different models: LU, RU, and HU (low, regular, and high utilities), having 17-, 20- and 24-inch clearance, respectively. Of course, each model had different rear-wheel equipment and matching front-axle spindles.

What I received from the Dubuque Works was a pair of hoods (one each for the 1020 and 2020), three- and four-cylinder engines with front-mounted fuel tanks, two transmissions (one with three-point-

Prototypes in the Making

Taken in 1965 in a studio at the John Deere Waterloo Tractor Works, this photo shows how prototype parts from two tractors were interchanged to create six different utility models. The author—thirty-five years younger than today—is standing behind the 2020 Tractor. (Ralph Hughes)

1962 John Deere 4010 Hi-Crop LPG
Owner: George Braaksma. (Photograph © Ralph W. Sanders)

hitch, one without), three different sets of rear wheels and tires, three different front-axle assemblies, plus a variety of seats and optional equipment. All of these prototype parts were delivered to a photo studio at the Waterloo Works where for the next month I used a wrench instead of a typewriter. Fortunately, the Dubuque Works provided two experienced service men who I tired to assist, or at least stay out of their way. With all of these parts, we assembled each of the six utility models one at a time, interchanging the appropriate parts as needed.

There was one advantage to this arrangement: It gave me an opportunity to learn all about these new tractors, from top to bottom and inside out. During this studio photo program, I saw first hand that the 1020 and 2020 tractors were not warmed-over or modified 1010 and 2010 tractors. They were, in fact, brand new utility tractors fresh from the drawing board. They also were referred to as "worldwide" tractors, because nearly identical models with different number designations were manufactured at the John Deere Mannheim Works in Germany for sale in Canada and Europe.

When comparing the 1010 to the 1020, many design differences were apparent. A 1010 with four-cylinder diesel engine had delivered 35.99 PTO horsepower when tested in Nebraska. A 1020 diesel with one less cylinder produced 38.92 horsepower at the PTO—nearly 10 percent more power. The 1010 had a sliding-gear-type transmission with five

1963 John Deere 1010 Industrial

Owner: Glen Knudson. (Photograph by Chester Peterson Jr.)

forward speeds and one in reverse. The more versatile 1020 offered eight forward speeds and four in reverse. In addition, the 1020 had a hydraulic Hi-Lo Shift that could be engaged on the go to reduce the ground speed in any gear by 26 percent and increase pulling power by 33 percent.

Furthermore, the closed-center hydraulic system on the 1020 was far superior to the hydraulics provided on the 1010. Hydraulic brakes were standard on the 1020 and power steering was an option; neither was available on the 1010.

Likewise, a similar comparison of the 2020 to the 2010 showed the superiority of the newer tractor.

***

The next task was to introduce these new tractors to the farming community; Deere accomplished this with considerable fanfare. If you have visited the Deere & Company corporate headquarters in Moline, you probably remember the small island located in the pond directly in front of the building. My job was to place a 1020 and 2020 in the middle of that island, so a camera set up on top of the building could photograph the scene below. This photograph appeared on the front cover of the December 1965 issue of *The Furrow*. A temporary bridge was built for the tractors, then taken away before the photo was shot.

That was only the beginning of the outdoor photo program.

1929 John Deere 2420, 1969 3020, and 1964 4020

Owner: Jack Purinton. (Photograph by Chester Peterson Jr.)

1963 John Deere 2010 LPG
Owner: Rich Rygh. (Photograph © Andy Kraushaar)

In the fall of 1965, Deere rented a CB&Q (Burlington) freight train with more than two dozen freshly painted flatcars. Securely chained to the flatcars were all of the new John Deere agricultural products to be introduced in 1966; this included the 1020 and 2020, plus new Waterloo tractors, new combines, new cotton pickers, and a host of new farm implements. The assemblage was photographed from the ground and the air, using both still and motion-picture cameras.

To obtain dramatic lighting, much of the photography was scheduled for the early morning and late afternoon hours. This meant that those of us involved had to board the train at dawn and ride the rails until dusk for about three weeks. The film was processed each night to make sure that all of the shots needed turned out OK; if not, similar photos had to be taken the next day. Throw in an occasional rain shower and delays due to other freight trains, and you have some idea of the logistical problems involved. The end product was called "Power Train '66"—some of you may remember it.

As soon as early production tractors were available, we headed to the field for yet another photo program. Photos were taken with the 1020 and 2020 plowing, discing, mowing and raking hay, cultivating corn, and loading manure. These shots were used in print ads and sales literature.

1964 John Deere 3020
Owner: Bruce Halverson. (Photograph © Ralph W. Sanders)

Cutaway illustrations also were needed of the new three- and four-cylinder engines, the variable-displacement hydraulic pump and the three-point hitch lower-link sensing system. Today, cutaways are produced on computers; in 1965, an artist had to spend several weeks hand painting all of the details to be shown in the cutaways.

Finally, in late 1966, farm visits were arranged throughout the United States in order to obtain testimonial statements from farmers who purchased a new 1020 or 2020 tractor. Although time consuming and involving much time on the road, this assignment turned out to be the easiest and most pleasant task of all.

***

The John Deere 1020 and 2020 are not yet considered "antiques," but they certainly can be classified as "old new tractors." In 1971, production of the 1020 and 2020 ended; the 1020 was dropped from the John Deere line and the 2020 was replaced by the 2030 tractor.

Today, when I see a 1020 or 2020 at work on someone's farm, I recall the month spent in a Waterloo studio bolting together six prototype tractors and my three weeks riding the rails.

Going International

By Don Macmillan

Englishman Don Macmillan is the dean of John Deere historians. Don has been involved in all aspects of vintage and new farm tractors: He started as a farmer before becoming a Deere dealer, and has since become a well-known collector of vintage tractors and involved with the English branch of the Two-Cylinder Club. His books include the landmark encyclopedia, *The Big Book of John Deere Tractors*, *The Little Book of John Deere Tractors*, and *The Field Guide to John Deere Tractors*, all published by Voyageur Press.

In this historical reminiscence, Don chronicles the rise of Deere as an international company.

1930s John Deere Model BW
(Photograph by Hans Halberstadt)

Unlike its two main competitors, Deere & Company largely remained an insular Midwestern-based farm machinery supplier until the middle of the twentieth century. Its only "international" manufacturing operation had occurred in 1910 when engineer Joseph Dain joined the Deere organization and with him his Welland, Canada, works, acquired in 1908 to build hay-making machinery for the Canadian market.

The company certainly had an export department, and had sent quantities of Model D tractors to Russia in the 1920s and had a useful trade with Argentina through a British import house, Agar, Cross & Company of Buenos Aires. But elsewhere Deere relied on independent concessionaires to represent them.

It was with two of these independent concessionaires from England that I traveled to the United States on my first visit in 1947. These concessionaires were director Dick Chantler and sales manager Jack Cromar of the Jack Oldings firm, which was the Deere importer for southern England, Wales, and Ireland. We flew on an American Overseas Airline's Super Constellation from London. We landed at Shannon in western Ireland for dinner; Gander in Newfoundland to refuel; and arrived in New York City the next morning, some twenty hours after takeoff.

Due to the terrific hospitality of everyone we visited, I delayed my return one week and sailed not on the Cunard Line's *Queen Elizabeth* but on the *Queen Mary*. This was fortunate, as Frank and Peter Standen were on the ship. The Standens were the importers for the six eastern counties of England. Both importer teams had ordered one of the new Model 55 self-propelled combines for customers; when these were traded in later, I acquired both, and still own them.

By 1950, it became obvious to the Deere board that sales of their machines in Europe were lagging

1936 John Deere Model BW-40
Owner: Bruce D. Aldo. (Photograph © Ralph W. Sanders)

far behind their two chief rivals in the agricultural-machinery market, International Harvester and Massey-Harris, both of whom had manufacturing facilities in Europe.

As a result, in 1951, Deere's Export Department, supported by President Charles Wiman, considered the possibility of building John Deere machines outside the USA. Encouraged by the British Labour government with a promise of a steel allocation in the difficult times in post–World War II Britain, a site was chosen in East Kilbride, Scotland, next to a similar factory owned by Rolls-Royce. Plans readied the stage that a company, John Deere Ltd., was registered in Glasgow; the firm is still extant. Foundations were laid for a new factory of 425,000 square feet to be built by the British government and to be rented back to Deere.

In Britain's November 1951 general election, the Labour party lost to the Conservatives, and, with their free-enterprise culture, they refused to stand by the steel-allocation commitment. Deere thus withdrew from the Scottish venture.

After this setback, Deere turned its eyes to a previous suggestion, and looked again at the German Lanz company based in Mannheim. With Charles Wiman's death in 1955, and his son-in-law Bill Hewitt's installation as president in May 1955, it quickly became apparent that the new youthful head of the company had ambitious ideas.

In a speech to branch managers within two weeks of taking office he challenged the old concept of Deere being a good number two to International Harvester; a letter from IHC had inferred they were not aiming to be runner up. Hewitt's response was that Deere & Company was not aiming to be runner up either—Deere aimed to be first in all business activities.

Combining
A Johnny Popper pulls a Holt combine across the Canadian prairie in 1927. (Glenbow Archives)

In this aim, Hewitt was ably supported by Ellwood Curtis, "Woody" to his friends. Curtis was a trained accountant, and Hewitt made him his vice president of the finance division and the company's treasurer. Curtis's financial skills and natural conservatism acted as the perfect balance to Hewitt's expansive ideas, and made the two a formidable and complementary team. The scene was set for Deere to start on its goal to become the world's number one farm-machinery company.

The first result was a trip to Mexico by Curtis, where he and the territory manager for Central America, Robert A. Hansom, agreed on the urgent need to set up a branch there. This Mexican branch became the first for Deere outside the United States and Canada. In 1956, it was further recommended to the board that a factory should be built to assemble tractors and simple implements for use in the Mexican market, and this was agreed. As a result Deere's first factory abroad was built in Monterrey, Mexico, the gateway to Mexico's agricultural area. In charge was Harry Pence, the executive vice president of Deere's export subsidiary, John Deere, S. A.

With his enthusiasm for a worldwide company, Hewitt returned to Mannheim in July 1956, some two and a half years after Kennedy's initial visit to the German firm in December 1953. Deere now purchased 51 percent of Lanz stock for $5.3 million, and so the second arm of the international future of Deere was added.

In 1957, Deere had started to assemble 20 Series two-cylinder tractors in a new $3.6-million factory in Rosario, Argentina. This was soon followed by four 730 models, the tooling for these being transferred from Waterloo following the New Generation announcement. A further model, the 445, derived from the American 435, but including five different styles, was added to Rosario's production line.

I was appointed Deere's first dealer in the British Isles in November 1958. This fulfilled the promise given to me on my first visit to Moline in 1947 to establish me as a dealer if the company returned to the European market. A visit to Mannheim was called for, and in 1960, my wife and I made the necessary pilgrimage to Werke Mannheim.

Two remarkable coincidences occurred on this trip. First, the young man who gave us a tour of the Mannheim works—including the foundry, which greatly impressed my wife—was Franz Odenthal, who later became the boss of the European operation.

The second was the fact that Woody Curtis, now senior executive vice president in charge of the company's finances, was in Mannheim for discussions with Harry Pence, the recently appointed director, transferred from Mexico, and now in charge of the German operation. And to set the scene further, Paddy Fleming, sales director of John Deere Tractors in the United Kingdom, was also there attempting to secure favorable terms for the importation of Deere machines from both the United States and Germany.

We were all four staying in the Palast Hotel in Mannheim, and so Woody invited us to join him for drinks before dinner. During our drinks, he was called to the phone to be told that Harry Pence could not make their dinner date as he was tied up with a union dispute over whether the workers could have beer in the works, an old Lanz European custom but against American thinking. As a result, Woody returned to the drinks party to tell us of the cancellation of his dinner appointment, and he extended an invitation to all of us present to join him for dinner.

To appreciate the subsequent meaning of this gathering I should explain that eight of us sat down to dinner, with my wife on Woody's right, Paddy Flemming on his left, and I was at the far end of the table from Woody. I am naturally tuned in to my wife's voice, and I heard her say, "The trouble with you John Deere people is you are so mean!"

I nearly leapt out of my chair, and Paddy, who had doubtless been trying to get some extra discount from Deere all day, burst out laughing. Woody simply sat there smiling with that inscrutable look of his.

1940s John Deere Model BO
Owner: Doug Peltzer. (Photograph by Hans Halberstadt)

But in 1972, at the Generation II announcement, Woody Curtis—by then the company's president—said he had heard I was coming to Moline shortly, and was I bringing my wife? When I said yes, he said he would be returning from Russia on the same day, that we were to stay at the Palmer House in Chicago on the Sunday and have lunch with him in the executive dining room at Deere's Administrative Center the next day. My wife had obviously made an impression on him.

Deere had had factories in Canada since 1910, in Mexico and Germany since 1956, and in Argentina since 1957. Now, in 1959, the company continued its foreign expansion with a tie-up with three companies in France, Rousseau in Orléans, Remy in Senonches, and Theibaud in Arc-les-Gray, collectively called CCM, or Compagnie Continentale de Motorculture.

The Rousseau works became the parts department for the French market, while the Theibaud works still builds balers and foragers for Europe. A new works was opened in 1965 in Saran near Orléans, France, to build engines, initially of Dubuque design. Saran also for a brief time made tractors similar to the Mannheim models, but with outside manufacturers' engines.

Further developments in the 1960s saw the Lanz-related Lanz-Iberica factory in Getafe, near Madrid, join the company's ever-expanding overseas interests in 1961. Getafe continued building the Lanz Bulldog Series until 1963, three years after Mannheim had changed to the New Generation models. The Model 505 was announced to the first Spanish dealer convention in 1963; it had a Perkins four-cylinder diesel engine in place of the 1010 Dubuque engine used in Mannheim's Model 500.

In 1962, Nigel, South Africa, was added to the company's involvement overseas. The majority holding which Deere acquired in the Nigel operation meant that a new company was formed called John Deere–Bobaas (Proprietary) Ltd. Later in the 1960s, the Bobaas name was dropped. Smaller tractors were assembled in addition to the South African tillage units already being built, and the implement line was added to with Deere's own products.

1970s John Deere 7520
Owner: Kevin Burbrink. (Photograph by Chester Peterson Jr.)

It was 1982 before the 41 Series of five sizes and twelve models was introduced, based on Mannheim's 40 Series but with ADE locally built engines; ADE were a Perkins subsidiary in South Africa. In 1987, this series was replaced with the 51 Series with an increase to six sizes and thirteen models. Tractors larger than the 3141/3651 models were imported from Waterloo.

From another initial partnership dating to 1970, Deere finally became owner of the Australian Chamberlain company in 1980. Deere built a special line of tractors in Chamberlain's Welshpool factory until 1986, when it proved more economical to ship tractors to Australia from Waterloo or Mannheim.

Like most of the North American farm tractor companies about that time, Deere decided in 1977 that tractors of less than 40 horsepower could be more profitably built in Japan; the result was the success-

ful 50 Series from Yanmar. The first models announced in 1977, the 22-horsepower 850 and 27-horsepower 950, were joined over the next seven years by six more models, beginning with the 14.5-PTO-horsepower 650 and culminating in the record-breaking 600-horsepower 11650, the most fuel-efficient tractor ever tested at Nebraska up to that time.

Subsequently, it proved economically possible to build tractors in this power range in the new Deere works at Augusta, Georgia.

In the 1980s, Deere held brief discussions concerning mergers with both Massey-Harris-Ferguson and Fiat, but these fortunately failed. Since then, it has been company policy to use other manufacturers to fill niche markets with Deere-styled and usually Deere Power Systems Group-engined tractors.

Since 1987, Goldoni of Italy has provided orchard and vineyard models in Europe. There were

1954 John Deere Model 70 Hi-Crop
Owner: Tony Dieter. (Photograph © Andy Kraushaar)

originally three models in the 42- to 60-horsepower range, all with mechanical-front-wheel drive as standard. These were soon replaced with four new 45 Series models from 42- to 67-horsepower. For 1996, a new 46 Series was introduced in Spain and Portugal with three models in the 20- to 32-horsepower range, and the following year the 45 Series was replaced with a new 46FA three-model Series up to the 71-horsepower 2446. The Goldoni line for Deere also provided the small European farmer with four-equal-size-wheel tractors, originally with seven models from 21- to 42-horsepower, four with rigid frames, three articulated. In 1993–1994, this series was reduced to one rigid-frame model, the 1042 and new articulated EURO 42 and 50 models.

Late in 1993, Deere came to an agreement with Zetor of the Czech Republic to market the 2000 Series as a low-price line for many countries. The Zetor line included eight models in two ranges: five

models from the 49-horsepower 2000 to the 81-horsepower 2400; and three models from the 89-horsepower 2700 to 106-horsepower 2900.

In France, Renault builds four sizes of the 3010 Series, which replaced the earlier 3000 Series. Carraro of Italy builds the four European 5000 Series models. SLC in Brazil makes mid-range Mannheim- and Waterloo-design models, and has recently been fully acquired by Deere.

With three successive chairmen who have all held the top position in the European zone following Bill Hewitt's worldwide lead, the company is currently involved in China, India, Turkey, and Poland.

With its overseas section still profitable, and taking number-one position in tractor sales in the United Kingdom in 1998, Deere is well positioned to remain the world's leading farm-machinery manufacturer into the foreseeable future.

CHAPTER 4

Sold on John Deere

*"I have not heard many farmers rhapsodize about machines,
except perhaps for ones they used during childhood—
two-cylinder Deere tractors or one of the early Farmalls."*
—Verlyn Klinkenborg, *Making Hay*

In the beginning, it required a leap of faith to buy a farm tractor. Horse teams were a tried-and-true method of farming, and the tractor was a giant step into an unknown future.

But after first trying a tractor, one farmer proclaimed, "It's homely as the devil, but if you don't want to buy one you'd better stay off the seat." No one since has so succinctly summed up the feeling of being sold on tractors.

"Clean and Shiny"
Junior washes the family's Johnny Popper in this painting by Donald Zolan. (Artwork © Zolan Fine Arts, LLC. Ridgefield, CT)

"Show Me" Three-Cylinder Happiness

By Ralph W. Sanders

Ralph Sanders grew up on a central Illinois farm where he had ample opportunity to "exercise" regularly a 1933 Farmall F-12 and 1948 Farmall C. Helping neighbors bale straw, apply anhydrous ammonia, and shell corn also provided working acquaintances with a Farmall H, Farmall MD, and McCormick W-6.

Ralph became a journalist, working for *Prairie Farmer* and, later, *Successful Farming* magazine. He is also the author and photographer of the long-running DuPont *Classic Farm Tractors* calendar as well as two thorough histories of farm tractors, *Vintage Farm Tractors* and *Ultimate John Deere*, both published by Voyageur Press.

In this essay, Ralph tells a tractor tall tale that "was relayed to me in the late 1970s by a mid-Missouri John Deere salesman where I was on location photographing utility tractors for Deere & Company tractor advertising. The salesman claimed it happened just this way. The names of the parties involved shall forever remain anonymous—not to protect the guilty or innocent, but because I've already forgotten them."

1952 John Deere Model A
Owners: Howard and Bonnie Miller. (Photograph © Andy Kraushaar)

"That blamed John Deere tractor you sold me last week has got only *three* cylinders!"

The red-faced, seedcorn-capped farmer was huffing and puffing to the local tractor dealer, showing signs of losing his usual quiet uncomplaining demeanor. The upset tractor buyer had stopped at his central Missouri dealership on a sunny day in late spring, an unusual timing for a "make-hay-while-the-sun-shines" operator that made most of his living doing a lot of custom hay baling in the county's rolling hills.

"You're absolutely right," the salesman cooed as he maneuvered to head off what he perceived as an impending revolt. "As I mentioned before, the Model 2240 John Deere tractor you bought has a *fine* diesel engine with *three* cylinders. Nothing is missing . . . it's made that way. It's from our factory in Mannheim, Germany. It's a great tractor! That's a really well-balanced, well-built engine. It's a three-cylinder 179-cubic-inch diesel. Puts out just over forty horsepower, fifty at the PTO. Shouldn't give you any trouble . . . it's running alright isn't it?"

"Yeah! I guess so," the balerman from the "Show Me" State grudgingly admitted. Then his voice rose, "but that engine has *still* got only *three* dad-gummed cylinders."

"Does it have enough power to handle your hay baler like I told you it would?" the dealer soothed.

The farmer grudingly admitted that it did.

"Well, if you can't get along with the three, and have to have a four-cylinder tractor, we can trade you up to the Model 2440, but it'll cost you more money," the dealer explained. "It's a bigger tractor with a four-cylinder 219-cubic-inch engine that kicks out about ten more horses. It's made up north in our Dubuque, Iowa, factory." The price difference was a hefty chunk more, he noted.

Conversation stopped for a moment as both men looked down at their feet and thoughtfully nudged rocks with the toes of their boots. What to do? The farmer wasn't looking for a place to spend even more money, and the dealer was sure he had sold the farmer the tractor that was the right size for his needs.

"I'll tell you what," said the peace-loving dealer who prided himself in making his deals stick, "why don't you try the tractor for a couple more weeks and see how you get along with it. Its three-cylinders ought to do just what you need them to do. Give it a chance! Then if you still think you really have to have one with four cylinders, we'll work with you. We want you to be satisfied."

It seemed a reasonable request.

The troubled custom baler reluctantly nodded his general agreement with that plan. "Guess it won't hurt to try it a little longer," he grunted.

Without further discussion he hopped into his dusty pickup and dissappeared out the lot and down the hill behind a self-generated hail of parking lot gravel and choking dust.

It was three, maybe four months, before the dealer saw the farmer again. Then on a drizzly fall day the farmer appeared at the dealership. He seemed all smiles.

The dealer tested the air. "Say," he asked, "how're you getting along with that three-cylinder John Deere tractor we sold you last spring?"

"Oh, just fine!" the farmer answered with a sheepish grin. "I put a tin can under the hood, sprayed it with John Deere green paint, and you know, I don't miss that danged fourth-cylinder one bit."

They both roared with laughter.

That proves, I reckon, that most of us raised on the farm during the Great Depression can usually still find happiness by making the most of what we don't have . . . even if it sometimes takes a little self delusion.

"Speedy Chores"
The Johnny Popper made quick work of farm chores in this painting by Walter Haskell Hinton. (Deere & Company)

"Autumn Memories"

Like father, like son: Junior couldn't wait to start playing with his John Deere once Pa had his real machine out working, as shown in this painting by Charles Freitag. (Apple Creek Publishing)

Friendly Deal

By Patricia Penton Leimbach

Patricia Penton Leimbach is farming's Erma Bombeck. Like Bombeck, she is a sage philosopher on the trials and tribulations of everyday life. She writes with a sharp pen about the joys and troubles, the hard work and humor, the meaning and value of rural living.

Leimbach was raised on a fruit farm near Lorain, Ohio. Alongside her husband Paul, a fourth-generation farmer, she has run End o'Way farm in Vermilion, Ohio, for more than four decades.

It is through her writing that Leimbach has become one of the best-known farm women in North America. For many years, she authored the weekly "Country Wife" column in the Elyria, Ohio, *Chronicle Telegram* newspaper. She also has three books to her credit, *A Thread of Blue Denim* (1974), *All My Meadows* (1977), and *Harvest of Bittersweet* (1987), all of which are filled with wit and wisdom culled from her firsthand knowledge of everything from raising puppies to driving farm tractors.

In this essay, she discusses the etiquette that surrounds buying farm equipment from another farmer.

Friendly Deal
Looking down from the perch of their Deere combine, two farmers survey the cornfield. (Photograph © Andy Kraushaar)

When a farmer buys a piece of equipment from another farmer, he doesn't call him on a Tuesday morning and say, "I want to buy that combine you got for sale. What do you want for it?"

He waits until supper's out of the way, then he calls the guy, gets his wife—"Howard around there anywhere?"—and finds out which of his several farms Howard's working in the early evening hours. Then he seeks out his own wife in the raspberry patch and says, "Going up to see Howard. Want to ride along?"

This is not the impulsive move it sounds like. It's a purchase they've long considered. When Howard went high tech and bought a new John Deere with all the bells and whistles, he noised it around that his old John Deere 9400 was up for sale.

The farmer's son estimated a price, run a cost accounting through the computer, and confirmed what they already feared: Their limited grain acreage can't sustain a combine profitably, even a ten-year-old 9400. "Going to cost us $400 more a year than if we hired it done," says the son dejectedly.

What he really fancies is one of those new models with global positioning and yield- and moisture-monitoring systems, intimidating all the people in his wake as he moves from field to field, waving to the neighbors from the air-conditioned cab. Well, the old 9400 would at least have an air-conditioned cab.

Dad and Mom have leaned back in the kitchen chairs reviewing the financial picture, considering the implications of this major purchase.

"Always take your chances with a custom combiner. He'll come when his fields are finished, and sometimes the weather doesn't hold."

"Like last year, for instance."

"Could lose a lot more than $400."

"Sure could."

But they don't make any vocal commitment to the purchase until this moment when he says, "Well, if we're going up there, we'd better get started."

Howard's over at "the home place" drying wheat. He's sitting in his pickup chewing the fat with another guy, waiting for someone to bring a load of grain from the field.

1953 John Deere Model R
Owner: David Walker. (Photograph © Ralph W. Sanders)

On Show

When the Johnny Poppers got a styling facelift by noted designer Henry Dreyfuss in 1938, the tractors became a star attraction at state and county fairs everywhere.

You don't launch immediately into the subject of buying a combine. That would defy the rules of sociability. A farmer takes his social life where he can get it, and a satisfying part of it is mixed up with his business.

There's talk of the wheat harvest in process. Howard's double-cropping, putting soybeans on after his wheat, and the whole process takes some discussion.

Then they have to hash over the big square ding in the door of the grain truck.

"Looks like the imprint of a straw spreader to me," says the farmer.

"Yep. Dad thought I'd moved and I hadn't. Saw him coming but it was too late. Got a new door to put on there, but didn't get to it yet."

They cover last year's bean harvest, the market prices, the rainfall, last year's rainfall, the tax bill in Congress, and the cost of money.

"Like to take a look at that combine," says the farmer, probing finally to the subliminal business underscoring the extended conversation.

They follow Howard home then along the backroads luxuriantly walled with field corn.

In the machinery lot out back the pair review the combine, dwarfed by its enormity, baffled by its green complexities, a far cry from the old Allis-Chalmers 60 that was their last experience of a

"Celebrations of the Past"

Deere tractors lead the Tractor Days parade in this painting by Dave Barnhouse. (Artwork © Dave Barnhouse/Hadley Licensing)

Above:

Orchard Tractor

A John Deere orchard tractor makes its way down a tunnel of fruit trees. (Photograph by Chester Peterson Jr.)

Left:

1938 John Deere Model AOS

Owner: Edwin Brenner. (Photograph © Ralph W. Sanders)

combine. They climb the ladders, peer into the hopper, sit in the cab, start the engine—kicking the tires, so to speak.

"What are you asking for it?" says the farmer at last.

They discuss the terms quietly, apologetically, for money is a crass thing. It could interfere with the warm kinship one farmer feels for another. They strike a deal.

There'll be a time for harsher words when the combine throws a rod or blows a tire. But in the soft summer twilight, as the fireflies flicker over the wheat field, Howard sees them to the car, and they talk of gentle things, of old times and family and the hopeful future. There's no telling how this purchase will end, but it begins as a neighborly encounter.

CHAPTER 5

A Love Affair With Green Iron

"We love old tractors because old tractors have souls."
—Roger Welsch

Many stories about old John Deere tractors are in fact love stories. They are tales of undying adoration, testaments of faithful devotion, and sagas of enduring passion. They tell of chivalry inspired by rescuing a tractor in distress, a search for the Holy Grail in that rare John Deere model or a missing part, and a feeling of pride that comes from running your hand along the hood of your Deere and hearing that engine thump along like a heartbeat.

1940 John Deere Model HN
Owners: Bob and Mary Pollock. (Photograph © Andy Kraushaar)

Old Farmer

By Kim Pratt

Kim Pratt is a writer and editor for *Yesterday's Tractors*, an online antique tractor magazine and resource website. The site includes everything from historical research to how-to advice as well as poems and essays about life with tractors.

"Old Farmer," a.k.a. Dale Jensen, began posting his recollections for *Yesterday's Tractors* when he was at the grand age of seventy-five. With an extensive knowledge of farming and tractors, he valued the past and the ways that went with it. He shared these values with the website readers until shortly before his passing.

The follow recollections are culled from Old Farmer's essays.

Happy Farmer
A farmer grins as he sits astride his John Deere Model B in the 1930s. (Photograph © J. C. Allen & Son)

The Day the Tractor Stood Still

Today I thought it would be a nice day to go out and putt around on my old John Deere G. I went out to the barn, slid the door open, and there she was. I went up and turned the fuel on, then pulled the throttle ahead some. I opened the petcocks, choked it, spun the flywheel twice. Then I shut the choke off, spun the flywheel and spun it and spun it until finally, half dead and out of breath, I was able to mutter some words I can't repeat here.

I was ready for another round, so I tried to start it again. It still wouldn't start so I laid in the straw of the barn floor, out of breath, and muttered some more words that I can't repeat. I then thought that maybe I had a dirty fuel system. So I opened the gas lid and it was bone dry. I almost killed myself: there was no gas in it! So I put gas in it and spun the wheel a bit. She fired right up. Boy, did I feel dumb.

I need to paint on all of my tractors: "Check gas before starting." I guess it's just age.

John Deere Man

I was born November 19, 1923, and was raised on a farm in southeastern South Dakota. I was born in a time when horses still worked the land and tractors were new. I was raised on hard work and in a big family; we had good times and bad times, but mostly good. My first tractor was a beat-up Farmall F-12. I went to World War II, came home, traded the Farmall for a John Deere Model A, and took over the family farm. I've been a John Deere man ever since.

Conversion to the Tractor

I suppose none of you guys ever farmed with horses, but I was just a kid and remember when we did it. What a pain! Those old horses would bite and everything else. Our neighbor had a big old Case steam engine, and I was amazed seeing it pull a ten-bottom plow. Well, we pulled our single plow with horses. Our other neighbor had a Waterloo Boy, and he thought it was the best thing around.

I was angry that we didn't have a tractor until one day I came home and I saw a John Deere Model GP in front of the barn popping. I was so happy I about cried. Dad kept the team of horses, though. He really liked them, and they could help with the work. We had the GP until 1937 when we traded it for the John Deere Model G, which I still have.

Our neighbors all got John Deere Model As after seeing how good our two-cylinder was. The neighbor's old Case steam engine was cut up during World War II. The metal scrappers took her away from the place, and his Waterloo Boy served as a backup tractor until about 1949.

Memories of the Farm

Do you remember when you were a kid on the farm, all the stuff you got yelled at for? I remember some—like when we had the John Deere G, Dad would tell me to keep it in low when I drove home. Well, one night I decided to be a speed racer and put it in full throttle. I put my foot on the governor, and boy, I thought I was sure moving along.

I was going down the road and thought I might be home before it got real dark when from over the hill came a pair of headlights and they were going fast! I tried to pull the clutch back to stop the tractor but I couldn't pull it back. Then it came by me, it was our neighbor's boy in his Model A roadster. He was taking the whole road, so my only choice was the ditch.

Down I went, through the fence and right into the hay field. I pulled the throttle back, slammed both brakes on, and used both hands to pull the clutch back. Dad sure was mad!

I also remember disking by the house, Dad would come out and say, "Quit lugging that thing around. If you don't know how to drive it, get off!" But I knew if I got off the tractor it would only make him angry. It seems like I was always in trouble.

I was either playing in the creek or catching chickens or chasing the pigs. I never understood why Dad would be so angry. But when I got my own kids, I finally figured it out. He was just trying to look out for us—that's why he would tell me to stay away from that picker or watch out on that tractor. He was just trying to watch out for me, not trying to make my life miserable

True Love

Those who farm together—with a John Deere—stay together.

The Demise of a Family Farm

I bought an old family farm back in 1974, about a year after I bought the eighty acres around it. I was just starting to get big in farming, and my brother and I were buying up all kinds of land. The farm I bought was the farm where my best friend grew up as a kid. They use to come over to our house and help with the farm work a lot.

The other day my son parked his payloader at that old place we got, and he told me he's pushing the place down but it's been raining today so he couldn't do it. So I went and took a last look at the farm. I walked into the barn and felt a eerie feeling

. . . I got chills as I could hear the old John Deere at work and the cows in the barn. I looked around and found an old pitchfork, probably the one we used to pitch bundles when we threshed. There was a lot of old stuff in there. I moved on to the old granary where I found an old corn sheller and the beat-up grill from a Farmall M.

Next I went to the feed shed were I found old tools and gauges from an old Dodge Brothers car or truck. The chicken shed had collapsed, and I could see the twisted pieces of tin that were once feeders for chickens. The hog house was still in good shape but the lightning rods had been shot. Then there was the small tin shed falling down where they kept the tractors. I went in and saw an old John Deere jack and a rusty back wheel from an M or H Farmall. The old workbench still had old parts on it. I then looked in the trees where I found the remains of a New Idea manure spreader and a 101 picker. Behind the barn sat an old Model T frame.

I went back to my truck and drove home. I started thinking about that place, how the family farms are going away because of selfish farmers like me buying up all their land. If I could do it over again I don't think I ever would have gone big.

When I looked through that farm and saw all the stuff I remembered all the small farms having old junk around. It was a way of life. Now, the big farms have new homes and big Morton buildings. But that's not the way it was back then. We all built the barn or the hog house together, everybody just farmed a small piece and that was plenty. To me it was a simpler way of life.

Regrets?

You know I've been farming for years and I got to thinking, was it all a waste? What did I gain? It's all a gamble, and sometimes you lose money. Like now, this year, we got acres of corn—and I mean acres!—and prices are down and there's no place for it to go. It seems like I should have done something else like be a mechanic on tractors or opened a tractor dealership or something. Instead I busted my back pulling out rocks and stumps to try to clear land to farm and turned it into a big farm that has so much land I don't have any money to farm it. I tell my brothers that we should get rid of our 8,400 acres, stop renting some land, and become a bit smaller. But they won't listen. It's all going to come back and haunt us some day that we killed small farms.

I wish I still had a small farm. I remember that everybody farmed a small piece, had a tractor, some

"Friendly Rivals"
A Johnny Popper meets a Farmall at the local farmers cooperative in this painting by Charles Freitag. (Apple Creek Publishing)

chickens, ten hogs, and fifteen cows. That was a family farm. When I think about it, it's like the ending of a poem I read yesterday: "we must keep with the times." You know sometimes I wonder if it was all for nothing. Did I do the right thing? Should I have been a doctor instead? Sometimes I wonder and my only answer is, I don't know.

Well, there is no going back now. I made up my mind back in the 1940s and I can't change that. But still I wonder, if I would have been a tractor mechanic would I be where I am now? If I were a doctor would I be rich now? I don't know but I think I made the right choice. I have a good a family and that's probably all I really need.

Saying Goodbye

This morning I woke up and instead of sitting in the house all day like I have been, I got my bibs on and my seed-corn cap and I walked out the door to the barnyard like I have done so many times before. I walked toward the barn and managed to slide the old rotten door open, and there she was: the words "John Deere" could be easily seen through the dark light of the barn. I walked up to it, turned the gas on and opened the petcocks like so many other mornings. But this time I couldn't start the old G. My grandson had to do it for me. He gave her two whirls and she popped and then a good yank and she came to life. She sat there at idle like she had done so many times before.

The familiar *pop-pop* brought me back to the days of my youth. I climbed onto the seat of the once-huge tractor and took it out of the barn. I drove it out back, and my grandson hooked the old disk up to it. I was off disking.

The old G was working under a load with me again, perhaps the last load with me as the driver. We disked for what seemed forever; I just thought about my life the whole time and just listened to the old G sing it's song. The popping of a two-banger

1956 John Deere Model 50
Owner: Herb Altenburg. (Photograph © Andy Kraushaar)

"Pitching for a Double Ringer"
The Poppin' Johnny becomes a place to rest at the end of a long day in this painting by Dave Barnhouse. (Artwork © Dave Barnhouse/Hadley Licensing)

Above:
1940s John Deere Model HWH
Owner: Doug Peltzer. (Photograph by Hans Halberstadt)

Left:
1952 John Deere Model G Hi-Crop
Owner: Bob Olson. (Photograph © Andy Kraushaar)

is one of the most beautiful sounds I have ever heard. I got done and drove her back to the shed. I backed it in, shut the gas off, throttled it down, and listened until its last pop had died out, like it was saying goodbye.

I slid the door shut and walked back to the house. I thought about the old G and it's last load, and how the G and I will be apart not long from now. I guess it was like kind of saying goodbye to an old friend.

Final Note: The Last Harvest

In August of 1999, Old Farmer told his many online friends that he wasn't feeling well and knew he didn't have much longer to live. He said he was ready to pass on, but prayed he could at least live long enough to see the last harvest. His prayers were answered, and in early October he was out helping his family in the field. His final moments came when he went to get the John Deere 3010 as his son got the combine. Old Farmer passed away on the seat of that tractor and was found later by his son with the engine still running. He was able to see some of the harvest he had spoke of so often. Buried in his old seed-corn cap, a twenty-one-gun salute was performed at the cemetery in honor of his service in World War II.

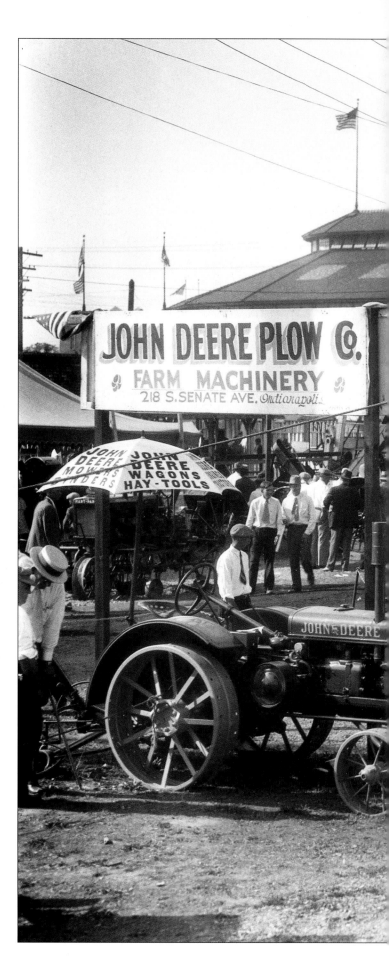

Machinery Hill
John Deere tractors draw a crowd at the 1930 Indiana State Fair. (Photograph © J. C. Allen & Son)

1938 John Deere Model G
*Owner: Lloyd Simpson. (Photograph
© Ralph W. Sanders)*

Phish-Huh-Huh

By *Justin Isherwood*

Justin Isherwood is a potato farmer and writer, a combination of talents as rare as it is profound. Farming has been the Isherwood family's livelihood for six generations, with three generations tilling the soil and tapping maple trees in north-central Wisconsin.

Isherwood's writings on farm life blend his sense of humor with a keen eye for observing human nature. He has penned essays on farmers' addiction for sheds, an ode to overalls, a treatise on farm dogs, and an examination of what he believes was divine intervention in the invention of the first pickup truck.

His commentary has appeared in *Audubon*, *Harrowsmith*, *Country Life*, and the *Wall Street Journal* as well as on National Public Radio. His short pieces were collected into *Book of Plough: Essays on the Virtue of Farm, Family & the Rural Life*. His 1988 novel, *The Farm West of Mars*, won the Wisconsin Idea Foundation literature award.

This essay pays homage to the sound of the Johnny Popper two-cylinder engine and the memories that simple sound can evoke.

"Grassy Hill"
A happy man stands amidst his collection of toys in this photo-montage by artist Peter Tytla.

I want you to repeat after me, the following sound: *Phish-huh-huh.*

Again please, with not so much spit.

Phish-huh-huh.

Once more all together.

Phish-huh-huh.

Say these words out loud in any ham-and-eggs, grits-and-biscuits cafe from Sandhill, Nebraska, to Mud-lucky, Missouri, from Dented Spitoon, Minnesota, to Wild Onion, Wisconsin; and soon after an old farmer will wander over and ask, "420?"

If you shake your head, he persists, "H?"

Shake your head again and he reshuffles, "G?"

"B?"

"A?"

"GP?"

"D?"

Shake some more and his eyes get wide.

"Not," he almost tenderly queries, "the Waterloo Boy?" It was the first tractor ever tested in Nebraska. On March 31, 1920, to be exact. Amazing it is how many farmers in hundreds of different cafes remember the date of the first Nebraska tractor test. March 31, 1920.

Course, what would a farmer who owns a WB be doing in a catsup-and-coffee cafe in the middle of god-forsaken nowhere? To satisfy the pained look on the man's face, "Nope, not a WB."

"Was it the 70?" You nod, and he wanders away content.

"What year exactly," he asks as he edges over to the coffeepot.

"'54."

"That'd be live hydraulic and power steering?"

"Was optional."

We had a narrow front as would uproot your jawbone if you were of a mind to hang on tight. Driving that tractor was sorta like bronc riding, somehow to hang on, but if the animal went for the fence, not to be too related as to go with it.

The reason farmers from Taterbin, Idaho, to Plowbottom, Ohio, have a separate reverence for *phish-huh-huh* is because that sound is very nearly the sound of a steam engine. Difference being steam was two stroke not four stroke. *Phish-huh*, not *phish-*

huh-huh. Meaning every time the piston went down the hole, it was pursued by a head of steam. When Deere & Company acquired the Waterloo Gasoline Engine Company in 1918, they did so to get the *phish-huh-huh* of patent number 550,266 granted to one John Froelich, who had improved on the unreliable Van Duzen engine, similar to the Otto, the Miatz & Weiss. For a while there, being of Prussian background was a prerequisite to the internal-combustion business.

These engines were stationary, whose intended use was to mill flour, generate electricity, and pump water. The Waterloo Company followed the horizontal—some say heroic—layout established by the steam engine. Having two more-or-less round cylinders, a disinterested number of parts, and a flywheel of only slightly smaller circumference than the great rose window of the cathedral at Chartres. Of similar design was the Fairbanks-Morse engine, which for two generations did everything on the farm from laundry to hoeing weeds and changing diapers.

The happy coincidence being there wasn't much as could go wrong with two cylinders, four valves, a couple porcelain plugs, and a thing that haphazardly mixed fuel with air, to whit that you could in a crisis substitute an old sock. The engine ran about the same. A wise manufacturer might have started out with a sock for a carburetor but that wouldn't have looked very dignified. To start it, all as was required was to roll the flywheel over and prime the cylinder, turn the petcock—yup, that's what they called the thing, a petcock; for a long time there were females who wouldn't ride a tractor much less go near one because it had a petcock—roll that flywheel once more against the compression, and the thing like as not started.

It was believed by many farmers that a male offspring could be trained in thirty-eight minutes to start and operate a Waterloo engine. Didn't need a high school diploma, a box of tools or baling wire, didn't need to know how to tie knots or the multiplication tables, or the difference between up and sideways . . . they could still start that engine.

Some believe it is this IQ pattern that has defined agriculture since Cain whopped Abel with a

"Spring"
Everyone enjoys the marvels of springtime in this Deere calendar painting from the 1950s. (Deere & Company)

hoe handle. John Deere tractors from 1914 to 1960 sounded true to the Waterloo, *phish-huh-huh, phish-huh-huh*. As genuine an emotion as was ever put to words in the history of dirt.

Phish-huh-huh is of course the sound of a John Deere at idle. Throttle up *phish-huh-huh* and it

changes over somewhere after the opening verse into a more normal mechanical noise.

The classic John Deere was always a little slow when it came to throttle. If you pulled the lever down on Tuesday morning, by Wednesday afternoon the tractor was wound up to the new setting. When

cultivating corn with a Deere, you had to anticipate when you were gonna hit the end of the row,
throttle off someways beforehand and hope to
Montezuma the cultivator pulled down the flywheel
in time to make the turn for the next set of rows.
Which is tough. However, before you got to the
end and before the tractor has yet slowed down,
you had to throttle up for when after the turn was
made, so as not to lose time waiting for the engine
to wind back up after you slowed it down for the
turn in the first place. Which sounds kinda complex. Which it was. And any who thought driving a
tractor looked easier than horse-drawn, went away
from such an experience pretty darn certain God
never intended agriculture to fit itself to the petro-
chemical industry as, like as not, render you a slave
to the internationals. That faction stayed hay-fired,
and soon after went extinct.

Farmers who made the transition to tractor believed Deere & Company intentionally withheld
improvements to the carburetor as might have offered an immediate throttle response. Doing so in
order to exterminate farmers who couldn't figure
out the intricacies of supply and demand. To arouse
from this clientele an intuitive sensibility about how
much to plant, so the bottom line came up black as
Iowa loam every year just like clockwork; if not
clockwork, at least like cultivatin' corn. The twin
cylinder opposed was an advanced economics
course, as much as it was a tractor. One taught out-
doors and with the demonstrative principles applied
by the engine instead of the college professor. Which
generally is an easier way to educate the reluctant,
the backward, and the sexually agitated.

Unfortunately for agriculture, there were im-
moral and fiscally irresponsible tractor manufacturers whose engines offered immediate throttle grati-
fication, by which any fool could weed corn without
the least bit of precalculation. In the long run, not
the kind of varmint you want surviving agriculture.
Besides which, these unscrupulous manufacturers

1959 John Deere Model 70 Diesel
Owner: Ed Hermiller. (Photograph © Ralph W. Sanders)

"Tractor Ride"
Junior's best friends go for a ride in the wagon of his Deere pedal tractor in this painting by Donald Zolan. (Artwork © Zolan Fine Arts, LLC. Ridgefield, CT)

used indecent paint on their tractors, circus wagon colors, whorehouse lingerie colors like red and orange and blue. Not decent corn and hayfield colors, meaning John Deere green. Besides which a four-cylinder engine is not blood related to steam or the Fairbanks-Morse, it was an engine you actually had to have tools to fix. Said of a John Deere that a farm dog with a pork chop bone and a bent nail could fix any ailment the horizontal twin could suffer. Carburetion being just a matter of washing the sock.

Some day there shall be farmers on Io, farmers in hydroponic Christmas ornaments floating serenely over the petro-rich clouds of Jupiter. Farmkids there will be some day picking stone in the asteroid belt and thinking themselves surely and truly damned by the picking of stone that never quits. Someday there will be other places where farmers gather, and the sound they will say to each other in greeting will be *phish-huh-huh*.

There will be scholars deep in hieroglyph and Dead Sea Scrolls who believe *phish-huh-huh* is from the pre-hebraic, ex-babylonian time.

They will be wrong.

Other scholars will object, saying the analog is very obviously Algonkian with emphasis on the Huron Confederation.

They will be wrong.

Phish-huh-huh will chant the Buddhist Methodist a thousand years from now thinking it a vernal blessing of the Bodi.

They will be wrong.

The hymnals will credit J. S. Bach, or Springsteen, or the Beatles.

They will be wrong.

Phish-huh-huh, will say and sing the farmers a thousand, and five thousand years from now.

Phish-huh-huh.

1939 John Deere Model BR
Owner: Robert Waits. (Photograph © Ralph W. Sanders)

1931 John Deere Model GP

Owner: Herb Altenburg. (Photograph © Andy Kraushaar)

"A New Farm Hand"
A grasshopper takes the controls of the Johnny Popper in this 1937 tall-tale postcard.

Left:
1934 John Deere Model A
Owners: Lester, Kenny, and Harland Layher. (Photograph © Andy Kraushaar)

Overleaf:
1952 John Deere Model A
Owners: Howard and Bonnie Miller. (Photograph © Andy Kraushaar)